The Unesco Educational Simulation Model (ESM)

Methods and Analysis Division (MAD),
Department of Social Sciences

Unesco

English edition ISBN - 92-3-101149-9

French edition ISBN - 92-3-201149-2

Composed and printed in the Workshops of Unesco
7, place de Fontenoy, 75700 Paris - France
© Unesco 1974, [B] Printed in France

TABLE OF CONTENTS

		Page
I.	The Unesco Educational Simulation Model (ESM), Development and Application, by Jan Auerhan and Erwin S. Solomon	5
	I.1 Main characteristics of ESM	5
	I.2 Methodology of ESM	8
	I.3 Evaluation of the experience	11
	I.4 Further possible utilization	14
	I.5 Non-formal education	14
II.	Data Requirements: Problems and Solutions, by R.R. Iyer	16
III.	Computer Application: Problems and Concepts, by Jacques Letouzey and Patrick Lutgé	24

I. The Unesco Educational Simulation Model (ESM), Development and Application

I.1 MAIN CHARACTERISTICS OF ESM

As any model (economic, educational or other), ESM is by definition an approximate and, therefore, simplified picture of reality. This has some important implications, which are not always clearly understood by persons not specialized in this rather technical field:

(a) Since models are simplified pictures of reality they necessarily have to reflect some aspects of reality and neglect others. By concentrating on some aspects, they help in understanding them. Obviously, the aspects of reality that are reflected in a given model should be those that are most important but the definition of what is more important and what is less important depends largely on the purpose of the exercise. Models have therefore to be designed according to the kind and level of understanding desired (not to mention possible). There are no universal, all-purpose models. (1)

(b) Since models are just an approximation of reality, they have necessarily to be supplemented by other methods and, more particularly, by the common sense of the planner. (2)

(c) At the same time, the real value of models lies precisely in the fact that they are approximations, since they make it possible to carry out experiments that nobody would dare to undertake with real systems, or that would be impossible to undertake in reality because of the considerable time lag or exorbitant costs involved. It is probably here that the major usefulness of models lies. (3)

As has been mentioned above, there are many different models, corresponding to different purposes. In the field of education alone, a survey published in 1969 by OECD and covering only OECD member countries and international organizations listed as many as 122 educational models, out of which 64 were already finished and 58 either planned or in progress. (4) Other models are known to exist in countries not covered by the survey and others again have probably been designed in OECD member countries since the time the survey was conducted. It is not the purpose of this paper to discuss, compare, analyse and classify all models, not even all educational models. Although such an attempt would certainly be very interesting, it would require a major research effort. It may nevertheless be of some interest to try a certain classification, which may help to situate ESM within a more general context.

Models can be classified, generally speaking, in very many ways, depending on the criteria selected and on the purpose of the classification. Leaving aside the obvious classification by major fields of application (i.e. economic, demographic, educational, manpower, etc. models) and remaining within the field of educational models, the following criteria for classification may be tentatively proposed:

---

(1) "... a model is a tool, and like any tool needs to be selected and used properly and carefully." F. Durstine, "Some problems and potentials of simulation models for educational planning", in "The use of simulation models in educational planning", OECD, 1971, p. 102.

(2) "Because models are approximate, the interplay between the formalized models and non-formalized common-sense approaches is always necessary." L. Rychetnik, "Macro-economic models for long-term planning and forecasting", in "Some reflections on long-term studies and plans: scope and methods", p. 124. Seventh Meeting of Senior Economic Advisers to ECE Governments, November 1969.

(3) "We can probe, experiment, and even attempt outrageous things with the aid of a model, to get an idea how these actions would work out in reality, without paying the penalty that would often be exacted in reality. A model, therefore, is a safe and flexible ground for experimentation, and therein is its principal usefulness." R. Durstine, ibid., p. 102.

(4) "Directory of current educational models in OECD member countries", OECD DAS/EID/69.79, Paris, November 1969. Restricted.

(i) What is the level of decision-making concerned?
(ii) What is the scope of the model?
(iii) What is the purpose of the model?
(iv) What are the mathematical characteristics of the model?

(i) According to the level of decision-making concerned, one may distinguish among macro-models (designed for national planning) and micro-models (designed for a specific institution, a particular project, a particular district, etc.). It should be noted - to avoid any misunderstanding - that a macro-model does not limit itself to treating all a country's educational activities as one aggregate but implies and can deal with any disaggregation (by level and type, formal and non-formal education, private and public, urban and rural, by provinces or sub-regions within a country, etc.) that is meaningful and important from the point of view of national planning (provided, of course, that relevant data are available). On the other hand, the viewpoint of micro-models is different and concerns either a specific institution or a particular school-district, etc. (1)

According to this criterion, the ESM is a macro-model and should be used accordingly. It is not designed to provide the level of understanding that is relevant to a provincial (or district) educational officer or, say, to a Unesco Chief Technical Adviser on a particular project. Problems such as the location of schools in a particular area, or the allocation of available resources within a school district, or the utilization of teachers and equipment within a particular institution, etc. clearly fall outside the scope of ESM and other types of models should be used in dealing with them.

(ii) As for the criterion of the scope of the model, it is possible to identify educational models that relate education to economic and social development, in the sense that the future behaviour of the educational system is considered as a function of economic and social development (i.e. of future GNP growth, of future manpower requirements, etc.) and autonomous educational models, which describe the internal relationships within the educational system itself. The latter can be further subdivided into comprehensive educational models, dealing with all aspects of the educational system, and partial educational models, dealing exclusively with some parts or aspects of the educational system (e.g. teachers' demand and supply, students' flow, financial resources, school building requirements, budgetary allocation procedures, etc.).

From this point of view, ESM is a comprehensive educational model as it covers all levels and types of education (including non-formal education - this problem will be discussed in detail later on) in any disaggregation that is meaningful for national planning and in terms of enrolment flows, teachers, costs and output from the educational system. It has been designed as an autonomous educational model in the sense that it does not attempt to derive educational development from economic or social criteria (this particular point will be discussed later on, in connexion with the purpose of the models). The fact that ESM has been designed as an autonomous educational model does not exclude the possibility of identifying some links with what may perhaps be called the "environment" of education, e.g. demographic growth, socio-economic development, financial flows, manpower considerations, etc. In fact some of these "links" have been tested already, on an experimental basis and will be discussed subsequently. The main point, however, is whether education can be considered merely as a function of economic and social development or whether it should be considered as an autonomous (or, rather, semi-autonomous, or relatively autonomous) system, having its own internal logic, although it certainly has some identifiable links with some other systems. The approach selected for the design of ESM is to treat education as a relatively autonomous system where links with the "environment", i.e. with other systems, can be identified, but where the development of education has its own inherent logic and its own relative independence and is not just a passive reflection of the development of other systems (demographic, socio-economic, manpower, etc.).

(iii) According to the criterion of the purpose of the model, it may be useful to distinguish between prediction models and simulation models. Somewhat simplified, it might be said that the purpose of a prediction model would be to generate a set of forecasts on what the system (educational or other) will be like in the future, whereas the purpose of a simulation model is merely to identify the consequences of changes (based on various assumptions or estimates) in defined conditions affecting the behaviour of the system (in the case of an educational model, these conditions will be changes in educational structures, introduction or prolongation of compulsory education, hypotheses concerning admission, repetition and promotion, changes in the distribution of pupils by type of education,

---

(1) For example, referring to the OECD survey, the following, among many others, would fall into the category of micro-models as defined here: Belgium Model 5 (Optimal location of new industrial high-schools for engineers), Canada Model 13 (Model for allocation of provincial grants to local school districts), France Model 5 (Budgetary allocations and students' orientation model for the Faculty of Sciences in Grenoble), Netherlands Model 2 (Description of the selection process of the Rotterdam School of Economics), Switzerland Model 2 (Teacher supply and demand model for the Canton Geneva) or United Kingdom Model 12 (Student Forecasting and Teacher Mobility Models for the City of London).

resource availability, etc.). Simulation models are designed to test various alternative hypotheses, to experiment with various options, to investigate, in a consistent and systematic way, their feasibility and their implications. (1)

Models attempting to derive educational goals from economic development targets would usually fall under the category of prediction models. Their purpose is to forecast what education should be like to meet some economic development targets. Basically, they use some economic criteria (e.g. GNP) as a predictor for educational development and tacitly assume that there is some more or less rigid relationship between, say, GNP growth (or GNP level, etc.) and the need for education. It may be noted that this assumption is not fully supported by the many studies attempting to relate levels of educational development and levels of economic development. While there can hardly be any doubt that economic development and educational development are related, this relationship seems to be far less rigid than was originally expected. This can probably be explained by the fact that education serves many objectives, not just economic growth.

As education serves many objectives and as the "hierarchy" of these objectives depends on a political choice it is to a large extent "policy-oriented" in the sense that the policy-maker has a much wider freedom of choice than in many other fields (e.g. population growth). It was therefore considered more realistic to adopt the simulation model approach for ESM. From a purely technical point of view, to design a prediction model for a field of activity that is pursuing multiple objectives is almost impossible.

A simulation model is simply a tool for tracing various alternative paths for development. It should be able to identify the various feasible growth paths by eliminating those that are not feasible. By adding a preference function a simulation model would become an optimization model and could be used for simulating the process of choice of the optimal path.(2)

ESM was designed as a simulation model which can identify the various feasible alternative paths for development, in the sense that it does eliminate alternatives that are impossible, given the actual state and the internal logic of the educational system (e.g. alternatives calling for an increase in third-level education beyond the possibilities of expansion of the first and second level of calling for an overall increase of education beyond the possibilities of expansion of teacher-training institutions or exceeding the financial resources available, etc.). However, a preference function was deliberately not introduced, for two main reasons: (a) the preference function for the different objectives is very often not known explicitly beforehand(3), and, (b) even if the preferences are clearly known, they differ considerably from one country to another and an attempt to design an optimization model would very probably lead to a whole series of models, more or less adapted to a particular country's situation and designed according to a certain possible preference. This would, in fact, be just the opposite to what was intended, namely, to have an operational tool that could serve at least the majority of the Member States of Unesco, if not all of them.

As has already been mentioned, education serves very many objectives. These objectives may be strictly economic (to provide qualified manpower in the right "educational mix" to meet the development of the national economy), political (to promote civic awareness and active participation in political life, or simply to satisfy the aggregate demand of individuals for education, etc.), social (to increase social mobility, to provide equality of educational opportunity to every citizen, to improve the quality of life and individual welfare), or cultural (to abolish illiteracy, to increase the educational level of the population, to increase the awareness of national cultural heritage, etc.). The choice, or preference, among the various objectives is a matter of value judgement, a matter of policy and, often, a matter of ideology.

ESM was deliberately designed as "neutral" to policy or ideology, i.e. neutral to priorities between educational objectives since it only simulates the consequences of various assumptions leaving the "preference function" outside the model itself.

---

(1) "There was much discussion during the seminar between those who advocated the need for a model to predict correctly and with a measurable precision the future behaviour of the economy, and those who believed that the important point was more modestly to reduce uncertainty about the directions in which the economy might move in an attempt to explore the impact of alternative policies." First Seminar on Mathematical Methods and Computer Techniques, Varna, 28 September-10 October 1970. Fascicule 1, p. 8. Economic Commission for Europe, ST/ECE/MATHECO/2, 21 March 1972.

(2) "... the criteria determining the 'optimal' programme are chosen preferences of those responsible for governing the society, based on their interpretation of the needs of society. These 'preferences' have the character of value judgements, not subject to empirical verifications, and are, in turn, translated - however inexactly - into the preference functions introduced in the optimization model." L. Rychetnik, ibid., p. 122.

(3) "It is often only when the policy makers are presented with information on the extent to which various policy alternatives influence the achievement of the objectives that they can specify their preferences." Brita Schwarz: "The use of simulation techniques in educational planning" in "The use of simulation models in educational planning", OECD, 1971. p. 22.

In other words, any preference, priority or hierarchy between objectives of education can, if explicitly stated beforehand, be taken into account at the phase of evaluation of the results of various alternatives, where it can be used as the criterion, or series of criteria, for evaluation. It is not, however, introduced in the model itself. This gives flexibility in the application of ESM.

ESM is thus no substitute for educational planning and, needless to say, it has nothing to do with what is sometimes called, with some exaggeration, "push-button planning". It is just a tool for the planner, which frees him from tedious and time-consuming calculations and gives him the opportunity to concentrate on the more creative task of analysying and evaluating the results of a series of alternative development paths, of revising the original assumptions in the light of the results obtained and of selecting the optimal path, using his own judgement and taking into account the priorities and preferences of the policy-makers.

(iv) Finally, from the point of view of the mathematical characteristics of the model, one may distinguish between <u>deterministic</u> and <u>stochastic</u> models. A deterministic model means that for each alternative path (which, for ESM, is composed of a series of assumptions concerning intake rates, promotion and repetition rates, distribution proportions, etc.) there is one and only one set of results. A stochastic model, by introducing the notion of probability, gives for each alternative path a range of results, spreading out more and more as the time perspective gets longer.

There is no doubt that, theoretically, stochastic models are superior to deterministic models as most of the social phenomena are clearly probabilistic. Nevertheless, ESM is designed at present as a purely deterministic model. There are two main reasons for this:

(a) A stochastic model, or even a basically deterministic model with some stochastic elements, is necessarily much more complicated from the point of view of mathematics and much less easy to handle. Since ESM was deliberately conceived as an operational tool that can be used by national planners and whose results can easily be interpreted by educationalists, it was felt that simpler mathematics may be an advantage rather than a disadvantage.

(b) As education is a rather complicated system in which all the interrelationships are not yet well known (e.g. the probability of certain changes in repetition patterns due to prolongation of compulsory education, or due to an increase in the salaries of teachers, etc.), an introduction of probabilistic elements may well not add anything real to the validity of the results while giving the impression that we have a perfect knowledge of the actual functioning of the system.[1]

The design of ESM as a deterministic model is thus more modest and less elegant but probably reflects in a realistic way our present state of knowledge and does not lead to exaggerated expectations. This obviously does not mean that there are not some probabilistic elements which could beneficially be introduced into ESM and future development lies along these lines.

I.2 METHODOLOGY OF ESM[2]

The fundamental concept and main part of the model is the study of flows of population through the educational system (enrolment). The other parts of the model (teachers, costs and output) make it possible to evaluate the consequences, in various fields, of the values of these flows.

(a) <u>Mathematical structure of an educational system</u>

In order to construct a simulation model of education, it is necessary first of all to define a mathematical structure representing an educational system. This mathematical structure should be sufficiently general to permit, without adaptation, simulation for various countries with different educational systems.

In general, it is possible to distinguish the following elements in educational systems:

the educational course;
the flows of pupils (or students) from one course to another;
the relation between populations outside the system and those within the system.

It is thus possible to take as a mathematical structure of an educational system a graph whose summits represent educational courses and whose arrows represent the direction of movement of population within the system and outside it.

This structure integrates two fundamental aspects of an educational system:

The static aspect: to each identified educational course corresponds the enrolment in this course. The state of the system is thus defined in relation to enrolment;

The dynamic aspect: the educational system is considered as being fixed during each time unit, which is generally one year. Its evolution takes place only between two time units and is defined by

---

(1) "... there is an ever-present danger with probabilistic models that we will use them to say little or nothing - but to say it elegantly - about the behaviour at hand ..." "... some probabilistic models do little more than formalize our ignorance." J. Coleman, "Introduction to mathematical sociology", Macmillan 1964. Quoted in "The use of simulation models in educational planning", OECD, 1971, p. 91,92.

(2) The authors wish to acknowledge the help of Messrs. J. Letouzey and P. Lutgé in the final revision of this chapter.

a set of rates which determine the flows of population within the system as well as the flows to and from outside the system.

Each step of simulation thus consists of applying a set of rates to populations to find the new values of enrolment corresponding to the new time unit, and consequently to determine the new state of the system.

This mathematical structure is thus a convenient support for simulating flows of population which enter the system, move through it and leave it.

It is now necessary to specify the variables and the relationships which define the state and the evolution of the system. There are two kinds of variables: static variables, the values of which determine the state of the system; and dynamic variables, which determine the evolution of the static variables at each time unit of simulation.

(b) Variables and relationships determining enrolment

As already noted, the educational course (a time unit of study - a year - within a particular type of study) is the basic cell of the educational structure; let "c" be the identification of an educational course ($c = 1, 2, ..., n$). For each course it is possible to identify by "t" the type/level of study corresponding to this course which permits the aggregation of enrolment to obtain global results.

Enrolment in each course "c" for each year of simulation "y" is further identified by age of students "a". For each course age-specific enrolments in a given year "$E_y^{c,a}$" correspond to the possible number of students in a particular age "a" in this course.

Outside the educational system, population relevant for entry, "P", is identified by age. It is possible to envisage several points of entry into the system (for example, to cover non-formal education) but the bulk of new entries into an educational system usually occurs at the beginning course of that system.

Two key variables have thus been identified: "$E_y^{c,a}$" and "P_y^a".

The entry into the system (i.e. the integration of population "P_y^a" into the relevant courses) is described by a ratio of new entry "$e_y^{c,a}$" ($0 \leq e \leq 1$) which will vary according to the course, the age and the year. This ratio, applied to population "P_y^a", gives for each course the number of new entrants into the system.

For the evolution of the system, the following rates are defined:
r_y^c = rate of repetition of the course c,
ϕ_y^c = rate of leaving the educational system at the end of the course c.

It will be noted that the rate of promotion from the course c is: $1 - (\phi_y^c + r_y^c)$.

The distribution of those promoted from a course c to other possible educational courses is defined by the rates: $d_y^{c \to c_1}, d_y^{c \to c_2}, ..., d_y^{c \to c_n}$,

where $c \to c_i$ represents the transition from the course c to the course c_i, and where
$$\sum_{i=1}^{n} d_y^{c \to c_i} = 1$$

The mortality which may affect enrolment is simulated in the model by applying to enrolment the survival rate "s_y^a" ($0 \leq s \leq 1$) in each year of simulation.

In each step of simulation the new enrolment "$E_{y+1}^{c,a}$" is a function of "$E_y^{c,a}$", the rates determining the internal evolution of the system $\left[s_y^a, r_y^c, \phi_y^c, d_y^{c \to c_i} \right]$ and new entries $\left[e_{y+1}^{c,a} P_{y+1}^a \right]$

The complete formula describing these movements is thus:

$$E_{y+1}^{c,a} = d_y^{c_1 \to c} \left[1 - \phi_y^{c_1} - r_y^{c_1} \right] s_y^{a-1} E_y^{c_1, a-1} \quad \text{distribution}$$
$$+ \vdots$$
$$+ d_y^{c_n \to c} \left[1 - \phi_y^{c_n} - r_y^{c_n} \right] s_y^{a-1} E_y^{c_n, a-1} \quad \text{of those promoted}$$
$$+ r_y^c \; s_y^{a-1} \; E_y^{c, a-1} \quad \text{repeaters}$$
$$+ e_{y+1}^{c,a} \; P_{y+1}^a \quad \text{new entrants}$$

This formula permits the calculation of the state of the educational system, each year, in terms of enrolment in every educational course.

The output of the educational system (i.e. the number of those leaving it) by age and educational course is: $\phi_y^c E_y^{c,a}$.

It is now possible to use the results for the following calculations:
demand for teachers,
costs,
cumulative output.

(c) Calculation of the number of teachers needed

Given the pupil-teacher ratio "f_y" it is possible to calculate the number of teachers needed. The ratio "f_y" normally is only specific for the type/level of education "t" and the variable for calculations will thus be "f_y^t".

Enrolment is known by course and age: $E_y^{c,a}$. However, for the calculation of the demand for teachers, the age distribution of students has no impact and an educational course is a too detailed notion for this calculation since a teacher can usually teach in several courses within a particular type/level of education. Enrolment by course and age has thus to be aggregated:
$$E_y^t = \sum_a \sum_c \chi^{c,t} E_y^{c,a}$$
($\chi^{c,t}$ = 1 if the educational course corresponds to the type/level t,
= 0 if the educational course does not correspond to the type/level t) which permits the calculation of the number of teachers by type/level of education:

$$T_y^t = \frac{E_y^t}{f_y^t}$$

Both enrolment and teachers are used here in full-time equivalents. Variation from full-time teachers or pupils (e.g. part-time) must be converted into full-time equivalents for the calculations.

Disaggregation according to teachers' qualifications "q" can be expressed:

$T_y^{t,q} = p_y^{t,q} \, T_y^t$ where $p_y^{t,q}$ is the distribution proportion of teachers by qualification required and $\sum_q p_y^{t,q} = 1$.

The number of new teachers trained in different teacher-training institutions can be identified as output from terminal courses of those institutions. Their qualification and, therefore, their possible utilization in various types/levels of education is defined by the kind of institution in which they were trained. It is thus possible to study the relationship between the number of new teachers trained each year and the additional demand for teachers between two years of simulation.

(d) <u>Costs</u>

The basic concept used for costing educational flows is unit cost, the unit being, for recurring costs, the pupil. Recurring costs per pupil are the result of identifying the relevant components.

$$v_y^t = \frac{F_y^t}{f_y^t} + \alpha_y^t + \beta_y^t + \gamma_y^t + \delta_y^t + \varepsilon_y^t + \xi_y^t + \eta_y^t + \theta_y^t$$

where:
v = unit recurring cost, per pupil
F = average teacher salary
α = per-pupil personnel cost, other than teacher-salary cost
β = per-pupil cost of general administration
γ = per-pupil cost of maintenance and operation of educational establishment
δ = per-pupil cost of books
ε = per-pupil welfare cost (school meals, etc.)
ξ = per-pupil auxiliary cost (transportation, etc.)
η = per-pupil scholarship and stipend cost
θ = per-pupil cost of instructional materials, other than books.

Recurring costs, for any aggregation of courses, is therefore:

$$V_y^t = v_y^t \, E_y^t$$

where: V = recurring cost.
Total recurring cost for the entire system is:

$$V_y = (1+i_y) \sum_t V_y^t$$

where: i = proportion of central administration cost (not attributable by aggregation of courses) to all other recurring costs.

In determining capital costs, the basic concept is, again, in unit terms; in this case the unit being a pupil place. Again, the unit per-pupil place capital cost is the result of identifying its relevant components.

$$u_y^t = \kappa_y^t \lambda_y^t + \psi_y^t \nu_y^t + \xi_y^t \pi_y^t + \rho_y^t$$

where:
u = per-pupil capital cost
κ = cost of site per unit area
λ = per-pupil-place area requirements for site
ψ = cost per unit area for building teaching and common facilities
ν = per-pupil-place area requirements for teaching and common facilities
ξ = cost per unit area for building laboratories and workshops
π = per-pupil-place area requirements for laboratories and workshops
ρ = cost per-pupil-place for furniture and equipment.

The number of places to be built consists of those necessary for additional enrolment plus those necessary for replacement of existing places, and can be expressed:

$$D_y^t = E_{y+1}^t - (1 - x_y^t) E_y^t$$

where:
D = number of pupil places to be built (full-time utilization equivalent)
x = proportion of existing pupil places to be replaced.

<u>Note</u>: It may happen that the value of D_y^t is negative, for example, when a particular aggregation of courses is being phased out. If relevant, an adjustment procedure taking into account a desired use of the surplus places for some other aggregation of courses may be introduced whereby the excess from one (t) is used to reduce the (D) for another (t).

Capital costs for any aggregation of courses is, therefore:

$$U_y^t = u_y^t \, D_y^t$$

where: U = capital cost and, naturally total capital costs for the system is:

$$U_y = \sum_t U_y^t$$

The summation of recurring and capital costs for any aggregation of courses is:

$$C_y^t = V_y^t + U_y^t$$

where: C = total costs.

(e) <u>The cumulative output</u>

The annual output of the educational system, by age and educational course, has already been described as $\phi_y^c E_y^{c,a}$.

Those leaving the educational system consist of two categories, namely those leaving upon successful completion and those leaving without it. This distinction does not need to be maintained here, since leavers are identified, within any educational system, by the educational course which they leave and a decision on whether they should be considered as "successful" or "unsuccessful" is largely a matter of value judgement. In any case, for most practical considerations, educational output has to be regrouped in a way meaningful for further analysis. For example, this regrouping can be in terms of manpower considerations.

The regrouping can be done in a way similar to the aggregation of enrolment (see above, part (c)), but the regroupment categories "t" may or may not be the same as those for enrolment. The aggregated output from the educational system "∅" will thus be:

$$\emptyset_y^{t,a} = \sum_c \chi^{c,t} \emptyset_y^c E_y^{c,a}$$

For analytical purposes, especially for manpower and employment considerations, annual output, even aggregated, is not sufficient. The notion of cumulative output is therefore useful. The cumulative output "∅C" represents the sum of the output from the beginning of the period covered, taking into account demographic survival rates:

$$\emptyset C_{y+1}^{t,a} = s_y^{a-1} \emptyset C_y^{t,a-1} + \emptyset_{y+1}^{t,a}$$

If for the base year "y_o" the initial stock of population by educational categories is known for all (t,a), the calculation corresponding to the above formula is not just a calculation of the cumulative output of the educational system but a simulation of changes in the stock of population by educational categories.

I.3 EVALUATION OF THE EXPERIENCE

This model was first developed in connexion with the Unesco Conference of Ministers of Education and Ministers Responsible for Economic Planning of Member States in Asia, held in Bangkok, 22 to 29 November 1965. It was first used to quantify targets for educational development for three groups of countries in the Asian Region, based on assumptions proposed by a group of consultants and reviewed by the Conference.[1] It may be recalled that the Third Regional Conference of Ministers of Education and Those Responsible for Economic Planning in Asia (held in Singapore, 31 May to 7 June 1971) noted "the remarkable convergence between the total enrolments actually recorded by countries of Asia and the targets laid down in the Asian Model" and considered "that the Model's projections for 1980 may, in general, still act as a guide for educational development in Asia".[2]

Subsequently, ESM was used, at a regional level, for projecting alternative educational perspectives in the Arab States, as a follow-up of the Third Regional Conference of Ministers of Education and Ministers Responsible for Economic Planning in the Arab States, Marrakesh, 12 to 20 January 1970.

Although those regional applications of the ESM were, on the whole, favourably received and successful (within the context of regional target-setting, an exercise which is in fact more political than operational), it soon became apparent that the most promising field for the use of ESM lies at the level of individual countries.

At a national level, ESM was first used in Spain[3] during the preparation of the Spanish educational reform, then in Sri Lanka[4] in connexion with the ILO employment Strategy Mission, in Rwanda[5] at a request of the International Commission on the Development of Education, in Poland[6], by the Polish Academy of Sciences, in Kenya[7] and the Philippines[8], both, again, in connexion with the ILO Employment Strategy Mission, and in Chile[9], in co-operation with ILO/PREALC.

These two regional and seven (to date) national applications of ESM have provided a considerable amount of practical experience. This experience helped to revise the Model itself and represents a certain basis for its evaluation. This paper attempts to evaluate the experience acquired so far by the Methods and Analysis Division, Department of Social Sciences, with the various applications of ESM.

These seven countries not only had very different educational systems, different educational goals and priorities and different levels of data availability, but each of these country applications presented some special problems for ESM. In fact, there was a deliberate attempt to conceive each country

---

(1) "An Asian model of educational development. Perspectives for 1965-1980", ED.66/D.33/A Unesco, 1966.
(2) Third Regional Conference of Ministers of Education and Those Responsible for Economic Planning in Asia, Singapore, 31 May-7 June 1971. Final Report, p.50, Resolution.
(3) Modelo español de desarrollo educativo. Ministerio de educación y ciencia. Madrid, 1970.
(4) Application of the Unesco educational simulation model. Study No. 1 - Alternative educational projections for Ceylon, 1968-1985. Unesco. SHC/WS/212, 24 February 1972.
(5) Alternative educational strategies (Rwanda), J. Auerhan. Unesco, 1971. International Commission on the Development of Education. Series C, No. 18. See also: Application of the Unesco educational simulation model. Study No. 2. SHC/WS/207, 2 February 1972.
(6) Polski Model Symulacyjny Rozwoju Szkolnictwa. Polska Akademia Nauk, Warszawa, 1971.
(7) Application of the Unesco educational simulation model. Study No. 3 - Alternative educational projections for Kenya, 1970-1985. Unesco, SHC/WS/1, 3 January 1973.
(8) Application of the Unesco educational simulation model. Study No. 4 - Alternative educational projections for the Philippines, 1970-1985, (in manuscript), 1973.
(9) Chile, Estrategias alternativas de desarrollo educativo, 1970-1985. Documento de trabajo PREALC/55, Proyecto Unesco/PREALC, Santiago, Diciembre, 1972.

case not as a purely routine and repetitive operation but rather as an opportunity to investigate some aspects not covered so far, thus testing and enlarging the potential area for the application of ESM.

For example, in Spain, where ESM was used in the preparation of the Spanish Educational Reform, the special problem to be solved was one of transition, during the period of projections, from the old to the new system of education involving a change in the educational structures. This problem was successfully solved but required some changes in the model itself, which increased its flexibility considerably.

In Sri Lanka, ESM was used not just for the country as a whole but for three sub-regions of the country and separately for both sexes. This again led to some programming improvements and, as a result, ESM can handle any disaggregation of the educational system (i.e. by sex, by urban/rural, by regions or provinces within the country, by public and private, etc.) provided, obviously, that data are available and that the disaggregation required is meaningful for national planning. Although ESM has no technical limits in dealing with any amount of disaggregations, it should be noted nevertheless that, for purely practical reasons, it is advisable to proceed with great caution in this direction since otherwise the planner runs the risk of being literally flooded by a huge amount of detailed results which he cannot reasonably analyse and evaluate.

Also in the case of Sri Lanka, an adjustment procedure was introduced to identify whether in a given alternative path of educational development equilibrium can be achieved between the demand and supply of teachers, within specified limits. The purpose of this adjustment procedure was to eliminate alternatives calling for an increase in enrolment which cannot be met by the expansion of teacher-training institutions. Although this adjustment procedure proved to be operational in the case of Sri Lanka and indicated that all of the alternatives selected were feasible from this point of view, it cannot be considered as a satisfactory solution to the problem. The adjustment sub-programme was in a sense made to measure, to fit particular conditions in Sri Lanka. These conditions (the existence of a considerable pool of unemployed university graduates who could have been drawn to teaching on short-term contracts) are too specific and do not exist in most other countries (even in countries with a problem of unemployment among university graduates the Civil Service Regulations do not always allow short-term contracts). In fact, to achieve a balance between the demand and supply of teachers, the mechanism actually used seems to vary considerably among countries because of different laws, traditions, employment patterns, rôle of teachers' trade unions, level of centralization of the educational administration, etc. The problem, therefore, remains open and considerable further effort is needed to re-think the basic logic of the adjustment procedure in order to find a very flexible solution that would possibly fit the particular situation of at least the majority of the Member States of Unesco.

In Rwanda and Kenya an attempt was made to include, under the educational activities covered by ESM, at least some part of the non-formal education: in all the previous cases ESM was used only for the "formal" education. The experience was very positive and proved that ESM can easily handle a large part of the non-formal activities, provided, obviously, that data concerning these activities are available, which was the case in both Rwanda and Kenya. At the same time, this experience contributed to a much better understanding of the direction of the further work necessary in order to cover more fully non-formal educational activities. This problem will be dealt with in more detail subsequently. In this context it may just be noted that, at present, ESM can deal with any type of non-formal educational activity provided it can be defined in terms of performance criteria derived from formal education or, in other words, that it can be considered as roughly similar to a certain type of formal education.

In Chile the special problem consisted of an attempt to explore the link between educational development and manpower demand considerations. It was envisaged that ESM could be developed so that it could relate educational strategies to the potential manpower supply which could then be compared with manpower demand, established by means of a manpower demand model. From the point of view of ESM, the exercise consists of the following: until now ESM has been designed to give results on enrolment, teachers and costs; the enrolment part also allowed the identification of the numbers of school-leavers by level and type of education as well as the cumulative number of school-leavers during the period of projection (taking into account demographic survival rates). In the case of Chile, an attempt was made to proceed somewhat further in this direction, namely, to calculate (a) future total population by age-groups and by educational standards for the target year and all intermediate years, and (b) by applying age and education-specific labour force participation rates, to calculate the resulting manpower supply by broad educational categories. This manpower supply can then be compared with manpower demand projections, again by the same broad educational categories, and, eventually, an alternative path of educational development, corresponding to manpower demand, can be worked out. ESM had thus been extended to produce the potential manpower supply corresponding to each of the educational alternatives. This can be done provided data concerning population by age-groups and educational attainment in the base year and age-and-education-specific labour force participation rates are available, which was the case in Chile. It should be noted that manpower demand considerations are, of course, just one of the many criteria for evaluating educational development. Nevertheless they do constitute, in any country, one of the possible criteria for evaluation in the sense that a certain proportion of school-leavers (hopefully identified by labour force participation rates) will have to seek employment and the correspondence or lack of correspondence between potential supply of and demand for manpower by educational categories may constitute an additional information factor which may be of interest to the planners and policy-makers.

From the above and from all the other experience obtained so far with the application of ESM, some tentative conclusions may be drawn.

(1) ESM, in its present form, is a tool of considerable flexibility. It can deal with any educational system, i.e. any distribution into cycles or levels, any length of the various cycles, any distribution by type of education at any level, including a mix of formal and non-formal education. In addition it can handle any problem of changes in the structure of the educational system during the period of projections. From the point of view of flexibility ESM does not present any major problems, its only limitation being the capacity of the computer. Since it can be programmed for any computer this limitation may well be considered negligible.

(2) ESM has proved to be a useful tool for long-term planning operations (10-15 years). It is not designed for short-term planning (e.g. 2-5 years) and for these kinds of projects another type of model would be more appropriate. In the short-run educational development is chiefly influenced by what may be called "the pipe-line effect", i.e. pupils already in the system influence, for a certain period, the future behaviour of the system. In dealing with short-term planning problems, a model based on extrapolation of past trends (and, therefore, a prediction model where time is used as a predictor) may well be a better solution. ESM was designed to test alternative educational strategies and, thus, the consequences of alternative policy decisions. Because of the inherent inertia of the educational system, of which the "pipe-line effect" is just one of the reflections, the differences between various alternatives necessarily only appear in the long run.

(3) The main and most promising field of the application of ESM is a systematic exploration of the impact of alternative educational policies, a description and tracing, in a consistent way, of alternative strategies for educational development. However, this requires that, prior to the use of ESM, the alternative educational strategies are selected in a meaningful manner, that they really represent alternative development paths and that they are clearly defined. In any simulation, results are just as good or as bad as the assumptions used and no model can produce valid answers if the set of assumptions used for a given alternative is inconsistent or non-realistic (the well-known GIGO effect - Garbage In, Garbage Out). The only thing that ESM can do in such a case is to eliminate alternatives that are clearly impossible. Since it does not have any preference function, it does not make any judgement on which results are good and which are bad and leaves it to the planner to evaluate the results in terms of preferences and priorities. It is precisely here that the usefulness of ESM lies. As in most cases it is impossible to judge a priori what will be the impact of a policy decision, what will be the long-term consequences of an alternative development path and, therefore, which alternative is "good" or "bad", ESM represents a convenient tool for the planner to investigate in a consistent and systematic way all the spectrum of alternative development paths. It is necessary, however, to stress some practical considerations. Although ESM can, technically speaking, handle any number of alternative development strategies, it should be remembered that the task of analysing and evaluating the results is quite time-consuming. It is therefore preferable to adopt the step-by-step approach, i.e. to start with something like three or four alternatives and introduce others only upon evaluation of the results, when the planner is already in a better position to select additional alternatives which would be closer to whatever are the desirable objectives.

This is especially important in the case of a considerable disaggregation of the educational system. To take a practical example, four educational alternatives for an educational system which is subdivided by sex and by ten educational sub-regions (provinces, préfectures, etc.) would lead to 80 sets of results, which would clearly be impossible to analyse and evaluate in a meaningful way within a reasonable time. In this case it may be preferable to identify, as a first step, the desirable alternative for the country as a whole; to proceed, as a second step, to the disaggregation and, eventually, to envisage a third step, revising some of the disaggregated results. It may be noted in this context that a disaggregation of the educational system is meaningful and worth undertaking only if the educational characteristics of the various subdivisions are clearly different.

(4) Another conclusion which follows from the above is that ESM can best be used in cases where a considerable amount of detailed investigation is required, i.e. for a systematic exploration of the various alternative development paths, or at least for long-term planning under two or more extreme alternatives. It is not a tool for a quick diagnosis and other instruments should be used for that purpose. From a purely practical point of view, although one alternative takes about 10-15 minutes of computer time, a country exercise with four alternatives, the educational system being subdivided in two sub-systems (by sex, or urban/rural, etc.), may represent, as an average, something like two man-months for the analysis of base year data, identification of alternatives, coding, card-punching, computer time and evaluation of results. By comparison, it would probably require several

man-years to do the same exercise using desk-calculators.

(5) Obviously it is not much use designing mathematical models that require input data that are not available at present and cannot even be made available in the near future. In this sense, models have to take into account the possibilities of data-collecting. This does not mean, however, that a model must necessarily limit itself to statistics readily available, in the exact form in which they are traditionally presented. It may well be that one of the important benefits from the use of models is that they help to establish and rationalize priorities in the work of the statistical unit by providing a deeper insight into which data, and in what form, are most important for educational planning. ESM does not, in principle, ask for more statistical information than that normally required for educational planning if no model is used. In no country where ESM was applied was the availability of statistical data found to be a serious problem. Although in some countries more data were available than in others, ESM proved to be flexible enough to adapt itself to situations where more or less detailed data were available.

(6) ESM can also be used for exploring an educational strategy that implies changes in the "educational technology" such as the introduction of new teaching media, etc. Although, from the point of view of ESM, this would simply represent an educational strategy as any other, the main difficulty in these cases may well be precisely in the availability of data concerning the impact of the innovation on cost components, pupil-teacher ratios, teachers' qualifications, students' promotion and repetition rates, etc. It may safely be assumed that there is usually not much sense in exploring the long-term effect of introducing new teaching media unless a measurable improvement in students' flows, or an increase in pupil-teacher ratios, or savings in school-building costs, etc. can reasonably be expected, since otherwise this alternative would probably only result in increased total costs of education.

(7) Finally, it may be stated, at least briefly, that in principle ESM can be applied not only "forwards", i.e. for the future, but also "backwards", with past data, to identify the probable values of some inputs for which no statistical information is available. This was, in fact, done in Spain where no information on repetition was available, to identify repetition rates corresponding most closely to the patterns of pupils' flows in the past.

I.4 FURTHER POSSIBLE UTILIZATION

Based on experience obtained so far, it may be possible to suggest, at least tentatively, some other fields where ESM may perhaps prove to be a useful instrument.

Since ESM was designed and has proved to be a useful tool for a systematic exploration of the impact of alternative educational policies, it can probably serve as a teaching tool for future educational planners. ESM, if properly reprogrammed and with easy access to a computer, could be used to demonstrate the consequences of various hypothetical changes in educational policy, including changes in the structure of educational systems, to indicate to future planners the long-term consequences of certain policy decisions and help them to understand more clearly the interrelationships within educational systems.

By the same logic, but as a research tool, ESM can, it seems, be used as a convenient instrument for what is called in economics "sensitivity analysis", i.e. as a tool to identify, in a systematic way, how far the future behaviour of educational systems is influenced by changes in any one of the parameters, e.g. ratio of new entry, or repetition rates, or distribution by type of education, etc. Experience so far suggests that these influences are far from being obvious and that while radical changes in one parameter may hardly have any meaningful impact, rather modest changes in another parameter may lead to significantly different results. It seems that ESM may be used to identify more exactly the extent to which educational development is influenced by the changes in any one policy variable, and to identify the policy variable that, under given conditions, is the most "sensitive".

It should be noted that these possible utilizations are just hypothetical and although they seem to follow logically from the experience so far obtained they have not actually been tested.

As a logical continuation and extension of ESM, a model was designed relating educational development to demographic change. This model, called the Demographic-Educational Simulation Model (DESM)[1] has not yet been made operational. DESM is intended to expand the scope of ESM to cover the following problems:

(a) the effects of population change upon educational development and policies;
(b) the effects of educational development on the educational structure of the population;
(c) the effects of educational development on future population growth, assuming that fertility rates and survival rates are influenced by educational attainment.

I.5 NON-FORMAL EDUCATION

As mentioned above, ESM has already been used (in Rwanda and Kenya and, to a lesser extent, in Chile) to cover, besides formal school education,

---

(1) "A model relating demographic change and educational development", Symposium on The Rôle of the Social Sciences in Population Activities, Unesco, Paris, 19-23 June 1972. SHC.72/CONF.13/7.

some parts of non-formal educational activities. This experience was positive both in the sense that ESM can handle a considerable part of non-formal education, and also in providing a clearer understanding of the problems and difficulties involved.

Before discussing some of the problems involved, a brief terminological note seems to be appropriate. In the context of this paper, "non-formal education" is used as a synonym for what is sometimes called "adult education" or "out-of-school education", and means simply any activity that can be characterized as:

(a) having <u>education</u> as its <u>main</u> objective (as against activities where education is only a by-product, such as production activites, or health activities, or trade-union activities, etc.);

(b) being <u>situated outside the formal school system</u>, in whichever way the formal school system may be defined in a particular country.

This definition is probably the least ambiguous - it covers adults as well as youth, part-time as well as full-time courses, people who left the formal school system as well as those who never entered it. For practical purposes, however, another restrictive characteristic should be imposed, namely, only those activities that are organized and sequential are covered.

The main (and most obvious) problem involved in using ESM to cover non-formal education activities is the availability of data and, even more so, their nature. Since non-formal education covers an extremely wide range of activities it is essential to devise some system of classification which permits their identification in a systematic and consistent way. For example, to know that there is a non-formal educational activity in Rwanda called "foyers sociaux" or in Chile called "formación para nivel medio" does not help much for planning purposes, even if all data on institutions, enrolment, teachers, costs, etc. are available (which is not necessarily the case). What is needed - in addition to all the other information - is (a) what are the objectives of this activity, and (b) what is the target population. A cross-classification of non-formal education by these two criteria would be extremely useful, not only for the use of ESM, but - it seems - for any serious planning operation.

Tentatively, the objectives may perhaps be classified as follows:

(1) Vocational and occupational
(2) Educational
(3) Civic, political and community
(4) Health and family
(5) Leisure and self-fulfilment
(6) Other

Target population should be defined at least by age, sex and educational attainment required and, perhaps, by sectors of economic activity (ISIC), occupation (ISCO) and place of residence (urban/rural, or by provinces, etc.), or any other meaningful criterion.

A cross-classification by these two sets of criteria would help greatly to situate any particular non-formal educational activity within its proper context. It may be noted that this problem does not arise in school education since both of these criteria are explicitly, or at least implicitly, involved in the structure of the school system.

Within the context of life-long education, this cross-classification seems indispensable, since otherwise it would be impossible to identify the mutual rôles of formal and non-formal education, their proper mix, their relationship, etc. Whatever may be the actual shape of life-long education in a particular country, its elements (or building-blocks) should be clearly identified.

Another problem is the one of performance criteria. It has been mentioned above that, so far, ESM can deal with any type of non-formal education provided it can be defined in terms of performance criteria derived from formal education. In fact, this refers not only to performance criteria but more generally to the smallest unit of performance and measurement used in ESM. Since ESM was originally devised to deal with school education the unit selected was a time unit, namely an educational course, defined as a year of study (grade) within a particular type of study. Correspondingly, any non-formal educational activity has to be expressed in these terms. This is obviously a serious limitation, since the flow patterns in non-formal education are usually far less rigid than in school education, and some of the non-formal educational activities (e.g. correspondence courses, or TV courses) can hardly be interpreted in terms of "year of study", while in other cases (e.g. part-time courses, which represent the most usual type of out-of-school educational activities) this interpretation may well lead only to some rough estimates.

Theoretically, it may be possible to devise some other "unit", and ESM could be adapted accordingly. This "unit" may well be something like "credits"[1] or perhaps some sort of "terminal performance objectives", if we succeed in defining them in an operational way. This would permit the use of ESM to identify the possible mix of different educational paths leading to the same terminal performance objective, and to select the path most closely corresponding to the country's situation and preferences.

---
(1) See, for example, Gretler, A. et al., "La Suisse au devant de l'éducation permanente", Lausanne, Payot, 1971, quoted from IBE CEAS No. 103, p.5

II. Data Requirements : Problems and Solutions

The Educational Simulation Model (ESM), mathematical equations of which have been described in the earlier section, is a revised version which takes into account the actual possibilities in data availability under different conditions. This model, in the revised form, has so far been applied on a national level in Spain, Sri Lanka (Ceylon), Kenya, Rwanda, Poland, Chile and the Philippines. The statistical and other informational needs of ESM discussed in this paper are based on practical experience in the above seven national applications.

The main purpose of the simulation model (ESM) is not to accurately predict the future but to simulate the dimensions of the quantitative consequences of changes in defined conditions affecting the educational flow so as to design a suitable strategy and the accuracy of the results of the simulation will necessarily depend on the accuracy and quality of the basic data used in the derivation of inputs. This does not mean, however, that the model application has to be limited to countries where all the necessary statistics are readily available in the form in which they are required. In fact, one of the indirect uses of the model is the identification of the nature and form of the data that are most important in educational planning. However, if the quality of the statistics used in the derivation of some or all of the parameters is questionable then the results of the exercise have to be interpreted with caution and can, at best, be of use in identifying the dimensions of the quantitative consequences of alternative hypotheses in educational planning. These will have to be further improved as more accurate data become available.

Before we go on to the discussion of the data requirements it is necessary to emphasize the importance of deciding from the outset the level of disaggregation at which the results of the simulation are obtained that is desirable for the country in question. The disaggregation may be in terms of sex, level and type of education, public and private, urban and rural, by provinces and subregions within a country, or any combination of these. This will depend upon the purpose of the exercise and has to be decided in consultation with educational planners and other users of the results. However, in practice, it will be advisable to start with a number of alternative simulations at a more aggregated level, say for the country as a whole, and proceed step by step to lower levels of aggregation, after selecting those alternatives that would be closer to the desirable target by evaluation of national results. At the same time, it is to be noted that a disaggregation at any level is meaningful only if the educational characteristics of the various subdivisions envisaged are clearly different. For example, disaggregation by sex will be meaningless if the values of the different inputs are the same for males and females and in such a case separate simulation will only unnecessarily increase the workload. The same argument applies to other types of disaggregation.

This implies that the alternative strategies to be simulated have to be identified at an early stage of the exercise so that the data requirements can be modified accordingly. These are to be selected in a meaningful manner, in such a way that they really represent alternative development paths relevant to the country situation. The relevancy of the alternatives will depend upon the immediate purpose of the exercise and has to be decided by educational planners or in consultation with them. It should be based on the different alternative policies in educational development open to the country. To elucidate with examples, in the case of Rwanda five alternatives were chosen to contribute to the investigation of the spectrum of possible future educational development for the International Commission for the Development of Education and these are given below.

<u>Alternative I</u> assumed the continuation of the current situation, with no changes in the educational system and the educational variables, to identify the consequences in conditions of rapid population growth.

<u>Alternative II</u> assumed the introduction of an educational reform, which had been prepared and approved by the authorities, to identify and analyse long-term consequences of this reform.

Alternative III was essentially the same as alternative II, except that grades 1-4 of primary education were assumed to be based exclusively upon audio-visual methods. An experimental four-year primary school course using audio-visual methods had been in existence in the country since 1965 and the purpose of this alternative was to assess the consequences of the introduction of audio-visual education on a countrywide scale.

Alternative IV differed from alternative II in that it attempted to investigate the possibility of providing the equivalent of eight years of education of some form to all children.

Alternative V was again the same as alternative II but with a higher proportion of children continuing beyond grade 5 in different types of out-of-school education.

On the other hand, in the case of Sri Lanka[1], Kenya[2] and the Philippines[3], the main purpose was to quantify the long-term effects of the present and likely future educational policies on educational enrolment and output for the Employment Strategy Missions of ILO to those countries and the alternatives were identified accordingly.

The ESM is modular and can be considered as composed of three parts: enrolment and output, teacher demand and supply, and costs, which to a certain extent can be used independently. The statistical data requirements can also be best considered under these three headings.

ENROLMENT AND OUTPUT

The methodological concept of ESM is to regard education as a system through which a flow of pupils proceeds. Hence the starting point of the data requirements is a complete flow chart of the educational system of the country. This helps to identify the different levels or cycles of the system (e.g. primary, secondary, higher education), the types of education that are provided at each level (such as general, agricultural, commercial, teacher training, etc. at second and third level) and the path of flow of pupils from one level to another, together with the levels and types of education that are terminal (on-ward flow of pupils from these level-types is not possible). Normally these charts are available at the Ministry of Education but they will have to be checked to make sure that the chart represents the complete formal system of education in the country. In some cases the flow chart readily available may not include technical or vocational education which are under the control of another ministry or of separate departments in the same ministry. In others the chart may be limited to the public educational system only and may exclude the privately-managed part of the educational system, which can be substantial. In many cases the post-secondary education may not include the part under the universities and higher technological institutes.

There can be some differences between boys and girls in the pattern of flow, in that some types of education may be relevant only for boys and others only for girls. All these will have to be collected and an overall flow chart of the educational system constructed. It may be advantageous to include also the non-formal education provided in the country and link it with the formal education system. For the purpose of the application of the model it may be necessary, depending upon the capacity of the computer, to group some types of education, in secondary and third level, especially if the number of types is large. The grouping may be done on the basis of similarity of type of education or, better still, on the basis of the values of the educational variables, which will be discussed below. The data requirements for the first part, i.e. enrolment and output, are discussed under the following headings:

(i) Enrolment in the base year.
(ii) Population projections and first-time beginner's grade enrolment ratio.
(iii) Repetition, promotion and drop-out rates.
(iv) Distribution of transfer from one level to a higher level.
(v) Demographic survival rates and migration.

(i) Enrolment in the base year

The base year can be taken as the latest year for which the enrolment data for all identified levels and types of education are available. The enrolment in all levels of education, by types and grades, is an input for the model. If the simulation is required disaggregated by sex, urban/rural or region, etc. then the corresponding detailed enrolment in the base year will have to be obtained.

The enrolment data available in the published statistical reports cannot usually provide all the details required. First of all, the data for the latest year may not be available in published form. These will have to be obtained from the statistical offices of the Ministry of Education. Even then they may not cover the data on certain types and levels of education such as technical/vocational,

---

(1) Application of Unesco Educational Simulation Model. Study No. 1 - Alternative educational projections for Ceylon, 1968-1985. Unesco/SHC/WS/212, 24 February 1972. ILO "Matching employment opportunities and expectations, a programme of action for Ceylon", Report, Vol. II 1971.

(2) Application of Unesco Educational Simulation Model. Study No. 3 - Alternative educational projections for Kenya, 1970-1985. Unesco/SHC/WS/1, 3 January 1973.

(3) Application of Unesco Educational Simulation Model. Study No. 4 - Alternative educational projections for the Philippines, 1970-1985. (In manuscript), 1973.

teacher training, higher education, etc. These will have to be collected from the ministries or departments concerned and the university administration. Special care needs to be taken to include the enrolments in private institutions of different types and levels, which may not be included in official statistics but can be obtained directly from these institutions if they are few in number or from the relevant departmental records or publications such as the annual reports of the institutions.

(ii) <u>Population projections and first-time beginner's grade enrolment ratio</u>

The model assumes that entry into the formal educational system usually occurs only once and is, by definition, at the beginning grade of education. The possible demand for entry is the population cohort of the entry age. The proportion of a proper single-age cohort which enters the school system (first grade of primary) is expressed by the first-time beginning grade enrolment ratio.

Generally, the legal age of entry into school is five or six years and the actual entry into grade one, especially in developing countries, is composed of pupils aged from five to nine or ten years. However, from the age distribution of the actual entry into grade one, for the last few years, the "model" age can be ascertained and, to simplify, this age can be taken as the age at which entry to grade one takes place. An alternative to this approach would be to construct an artificial "cohort" of a corresponding proportion of five-year olds, six-year olds, seven-year olds, etc. However, it can easily be demonstrated that the size of this artificial "cohort" would not differ in any meaningful way from the size of the "model" age cohort since first-time entry into the school system can obviously occur only once and those entering school at the age of five, for example, are no more relevant for first-time enrolment when they reach age six, etc.

For the base year, the new entrants to the first-grade in that year divided by the population of "model" entry age gives the first-time beginning grade enrolment ratio. The number of new entrants to the first grade is not the same as the enrolment in the first grade as the enrolment figures include not only the new entrants but also the repeaters from earlier cohorts. The enrolment figures have to be adjusted for the repeaters to obtain the new entrants, if the new entrant figures are not separately available.

Once the first-time beginning grade enrolment ratio for the base year has been obtained, this has to be projected until the end of the period of simulation, taking into account the past rate of growth of this ratio, the educational policy of the country on primary education and other relevant factors. Needless to say, if the simulation is to be done at a disaggregated level the enrolment ratio has also to be obtained for the level of disaggregation envisaged.

The single-year population of the country is another input. The single-year school age population for each year from the base year up to the end of the projection period is necessary. Usually these projections are available from the census authorities of the country. Four variants of population projections, namely "low", "medium", "high" and "constant" fertility rates have been prepared by the United Nations Population Division for all countries. Any one of these population projections can be used in the simulation. However, the choice will depend on the purpose of the simulation exercise. If the purpose of the exercise is to bring out the effect of different population growth rates on educational enrolment, or output or cost, then separate simulations will have to be done using all or at least two ("low" and "high") of the population projections. However, if the main purpose of the exercise is to simulate the consequences of alternative educational strategies, then only one population alternative need be used, which is usually the "medium" alternative. Usually, population projections are available by five-year age groups and at five-year intervals. The population for each single year of the simulation period can be estimated by linear interpolation. The single-age population for the relevant school-going ages can be arrived at by using "Sprague multipliers".

(iii) <u>Repetition, promotion and drop-out rates</u>

The flow of pupils through the system is identified in the model by the following criteria: a pupil repeats the same grade the following year, he proceeds (promoted) to another grade or course the following year, or he leaves the system. Of those who leave the system a further identification is made, namely, those who leave upon successful completion and those who leave without successful completion (commonly referred to as drop-outs). However, the model does not separately identify the school-leavers into "successful" and "unsuccessful" leavers. Those who leave the system at the end of an educational cycle are taken as corresponding to the successful leavers and those who leave at other grades as unsuccessful leavers or drop-outs. The repetition, promotion and leaving rates measure these aspects of student flow.

The <u>repetition rate</u> is the proportion of repeaters in a given grade to the total enrolment in that grade the previous year, i.e.

$$r_y^g = \frac{R_y^{g+1}}{E_y^g} \; ; \quad \text{where } r = \text{repetition rate}$$
$$R = \text{No. of repeaters}$$
$$E = \text{enrolment, and } g \text{ and } y$$
$$\text{stand for grade and year.}$$

The <u>leaving rate</u> is the proportion of pupils leaving the system in a given grade in a given year to the enrolment in that grade in that year, i.e.

$$l_y^g = \frac{L_y^g}{E_y^g} \quad \text{where } l = \text{leaving rate (successful + unsuccessful)}$$
$$L = \text{No. of pupils leaving the system.}$$

The promotion rate can be obtained as a residual since
$$p_y^g + r_y^g + l_y^g = 1.$$
It is to be noted that those pupils who successfully complete a grade but do not continue in the educational system are not included in those who are "promoted" but form a part of the school-leavers and are identified separately as "successful school-leavers".

For the base year, data on repetition rates and leaving rates are to be obtained for the different types of education, for each level and grade. If the simulation is being disaggregated by sex or urban/rural areas, etc. then the repetition rates and leaving rates are to be obtained disaggregated by sex and urban/rural areas.

Generally, repetition and leaving rates for the different educational levels, types and grades are not available in many developing countries. In some cases the relevant data are systematically collected only for first and second level education and that too is not disaggregated by type of education, sex, etc. Even though systematic data on these aspects are not collected it is possible that relevant data are available, based on special studies that have been carried out for specific purposes by the departments or research organizations concerned.

If no such data exist, approximate values of these rates can be calculated from an analysis of past enrolment data by types, levels and grades. The ratios thus obtained can be used as a first approximation and can be improved by successive approximation with the use of the model 'backwards" to the past data, so that these rates correspond most closely to the pattern of pupil flows. This method was, in fact, adopted in Spain where no information on repetition was available.

The base year rates have also to be projected for each year of simulation, depending upon the assumptions of the different alternatives under simulation. This will have to be done taking into account the future policy of the country which may affect these variables. Alternative target rates for some years may be available from the educational plans of the country or can be ascertained by discussion with the authorities concerned.

(iv) <u>Distribution of transfer from one level to a higher level</u>

In a particular cycle of education, the pupils who are promoted from any grade other than the last grade and continue in the educational system proceed to the next higher grade in the same cycle but those who are promoted from the last grade of a cycle and continue in the system have the possibility of proceeding to different types of education in the next higher cycle. Therefore, to follow the flow of promotions through the system it is necessary to know their distribution in the next cycle among the different possible types of courses such as arts, science, agriculture, engineering, etc. Such distribution takes place in the case of all cycles, excepting those that are terminal and so from which onward flow into other levels of education is not possible. In the model this distribution among different possible types of courses is identified by the distribution proportion d_y^c.

The data on distribution proportion are to be calculated or estimated for every cycle in the educational system, where the possibility of flow into alternative courses exists. For the base year this distribution proportion can be calculated on the basis of an analysis of the enrolment in the beginning grade of the relevant types of courses, after adjusting for the repeaters. The total of the adjusted enrolment will give the total number of promoters and the adjusted enrolment in each type as a proportion of the total in all the types will give the distribution proportion in each type. It will be useful to calculate this distribution proportion, not only for the base year but also for a number of past years to examine the trends. The distribution proportion to each type of course for each year of the simulation period has to be estimated. This will mainly be based on the policy in this respect. If the policy is to continue the existing trends then a detailed study of the past trends becomes very important and this has to be extrapolated up to the end of the simulation period, using suitable formulae. However, usually the policy will be not to continue the current trends but to change the distribution in favour of some types of study, e.g. technical, technological and scientific courses. In such cases the distribution proportions for the different courses have to be estimated for each year based on policies in this respect or based on other practical considerations.

(v) <u>Demographic survival rates and migration</u>

Another parameter that has been identified in the model is the demographic survival rates (S_y). A certain number of the pupils who enter the educational system die as they pass through the system and the demographic survival rates are used to take account of this natural phenomenon. The demographic survival rates are required also to obtain cumulative stock of educational output during specified periods, say, at the end of every five years.

For countries where regular population censuses or surveys are conducted or where vital registration data are available these rates can be obtained from the life tables (column headed $_nP_x$). Usually these rates are available in five-year intervals and can be interpolated suitably to obtain the survival rates corresponding to single-year ages. For countries where such data do not exist the survival rates may be obtained from suitable United Nations model life tables or from the life tables of countries with similar mortality experience. However, in practice, in countries where the mortality rates for the school-age population (ages 5-24) are not substantial the omission of this factor from the model will not affect the results seriously. Even then this information will be necessary to obtain the mortality-adjusted cumulative output in different future years.

Another factor, which is taken into account in the model, is the migration of students. The necessity for accurate data on the migration of students becomes more important if the simulation is attempted on a regional basis, i.e. by provinces or districts or by urban/rural, etc. This is so because migration of students from one country to another is not usually significant. However, in countries where regional institutions are located or in those countries that participate substantially in regional institutions situated in another country in the region migration of students at the relevant levels can be important and has to be taken into account. But migration of students within a country from State to State or region to region is very important.

At the national level, migration of students can be of some importance at the higher educational level. Depending upon the development of higher education facilities in the country, students will be immigrating for further studies. The number of net migrants to the system, classified by type and level, is the required input. It is possible to obtain the information from the records of the Ministry of Education which give the number of students, by type of study, going abroad for studies and the number who enter the country for studies.

For simulation by regions, or rural/urban, etc., the net migration data required will cover all the levels, types and grades since between regions and between rural/urban areas of a country migration is more numerous than migration between countries. Moreover, these data are more difficult to obtain because such data are not available consolidated at the national level. Special studies will have to be conducted to obtain the necessary information, which may not be possible within a short time. However, in studies on the application of the model undertaken up until now no account was taken of migration because all, with the exception of Sri Lanka, were at the national level, and in the case of Sri Lanka no reliable data on internal migration were available.

TEACHER DEMAND AND SUPPLY

This part of the model simulates the teacher requirements for the various alternative simulations of enrolment, under different alternative teacher use patterns. The total stock of teachers needed in any year is calculated by linking it to enrolment through pupil/teacher ratios (f). The model is flexible enough to utilize more detailed data if available. The teacher requirements can be disaggregated by qualification, if in addition the distribution proportion of teachers by qualification can be obtained. Further, to estimate additional teacher requirements in one year, the demographic survival rates, retirement rates, leaving rates of teachers to other professions, and entry rate into teaching from other professions are required. At any rate, estimation of additional teacher requirements was not attempted in any of the exercises done until now.

For the base year, the pupil/teacher ratio for different levels and types of education can be calculated from the data on enrolment and the stock of teachers, which are readily available. The number of teachers and the enrolment have to be in terms of full-time equivalents. The part-time teachers and the part-time pupils have to be converted into full-time equivalents on the basis of information on the time disposition of part-time teachers and pupils, which may be ascertained by discussion with concerned authorities if not already documented. In the case of technical and vocational education and higher education, the relevant data may not be available in the official statistics of the ministries of education and may have to be obtained from the relevant departments and university administration. There can be wide differences in the pupil/teacher ratio between public and private institutions and also between institutions in urban and rural areas.

The data on distribution of teachers by qualifications for different levels and types of education are more difficult to come across. The teachers, especially in general primary and secondary education, are classified not only by their general educational qualifications but also by whether they are trained teachers or not. This distribution can be obtained from the records of the ministries of education. In countries where this is not collected, existence of such data based on some special studies or surveys may be explored, to be used to estimate the likely distribution. This is also an aspect of the model which has not yet been applied in any country situation but is expected to be of use in the future.

Once the base year pupil/teacher ratio, distribution proportion of teachers, etc. have been arrived at, these have to be projected for each year of the simulation period. This has to be done on the basis of the educational targets for these parameters which might already have been fixed in the national development plans or based on the general policy of the country. In some cases the ultimate target rates can be fixed based on international standards and for the intermediate years the figures can be calculated by interpolation in such a way that the target rates are achieved gradually.

The total stock of teachers and the annual teacher requirements simulated for the different alternatives give the corresponding demand for teachers. The corresponding supply will be available from the educational output in the first part of the exercise. The educational output in one year will be available as teachers in the next year.

Of course, the available number of teachers will depend on the labour force participation rates of the output. There has to be a balance between teacher requirements and teacher output. The imbalance can occur in two ways: (i) the output is in excess of the demand, (ii) the demand is in excess of the supply.

In the case of output being in excess of the demand, the enrolment simulation can be adjusted, in a second run, by suitably changing the corresponding distribution proportion going into the type of teacher education which is in excess, such that the demand and supply match to the expected degree. Alternatively, the corresponding pupil/teacher ratio can be decreased, in the simulation of teacher requirements, so that the two figures match.

Similarly, in the case where the demand is in excess of supply, there are various ways in which the matching can be accomplished. One alternative is to increase the pupil/teacher ratio if it is practicable in reality to the extent that there will be excess demand. Another possibility is to increase the corresponding output by suitably increasing the transfer rates or decreasing the repetition and unsuccessful leaving in the earlier grades. The priority and adjustment procedures to be followed will depend on the particular situation and practical possibilities. By such suitable adjustments the results of the simulation can be improved so that the demand and supply of teachers match to the degree required.

EDUCATIONAL COSTS

The third part of the educational simulation model is the costing of educational flows. Alternative cost patterns can be simulated through this part of the model, corresponding to each of the alternative simulations of the educational flows of the first part. Educational costs here include recurring costs and capital costs and these two are simulated independently.

(a) Recurring costs

The basic concept used for costing educational flows is the unit cost. In the case of recurring costs, the unit is the pupil. Recurring cost per pupil are the total of cost per pupil of relevant identified components. The model is flexible enough to accommodate the different country situations on the availability of data and the number of components which can be separately identified.

The model has identified the following as the constituents of the recurring cost:

(i) Teacher salary
(ii) Personnel cost, other than teacher salary
(iii) General Administration
(iv) Maintenance and operation of educational establishment
(v) Books
(vi) Welfare (school meals, uniforms, etc.)
(vii) Auxiliary (transportation, health care, etc.)
(viii) Scholarship and stipend
(ix) Instructional materials, other than books
(x) Central administration (not attributable by aggregation of courses).

The above list is only illustrative of the items which may be taken into account in the calculation of recurring costs. It in no way means that all these items in the form listed above have to be taken into account. The number of items and their nature will depend upon the availability of data in particular situations. If, for example, in a particular country the data are available only on teachers' salaries and all other costs put together, even then the model can use these data to arrive at the recurring costs for the system. However, it is worth mentioning that it is better to break down the total per pupil cost into as many components as possible, depending upon the availability of data.

Teacher salary. Teacher salary forms a major part of the total recurring cost for all levels and types of education. In the case of first level education it usually forms about 80% of the total recurring cost and its percentage contribution decreases as the level of education rises.

Average teaching salary classified by the level of disaggregation envisaged is the required input for the model, i.e. average teacher salary by level and type of education for the country as a whole or classified by rural and urban areas, public and private institutions, etc. The average teacher salary for a particular level and type of education divided by the pupil-teacher ratio gives the per-pupil teacher cost.

The sources of information on teacher salaries are the following:

1. Statistics of educational expenditure classified by items of expenditure, identified separately, include teachers' salaries. This data if available classified by type and level of institutions will be the best source of information for all types of institutions and managements. The total salary expenditure divided by the corresponding number of teachers will give the average teacher salary.

2. The annual budget estimates of the concerned ministries and universities show the actual and anticipated expenditure for the previous year and current year, respectively, on teachers' salaries, together with the number of teachers by types and levels of educational institutions. This information can be used to estimate the average teacher salary of teachers in public schools.

3. The existing pay scales of teachers, by qualification in different levels and types of institutions, are sometimes available in published form or can be obtained from records of the ministries of education, universities, etc. These may also be available from recent reports of commissions

on pay revision, etc. These data may cover both public and private institutions or only public. If, in addition, the average length of service of teachers is available, the average basic teacher salary can be estimated. To this should be added the allowances, including pension contribution, etc. to arrive at the average teacher cost.

4. Estimates of average teacher salaries of different qualifications and levels and types of education may be available in special studies and surveys conducted for specific purposes.

It may not be possible to obtain the needed information for all levels and types of institution from any one source. Information from all sources listed above could be used to arrive at the needed data and to cross-check it. Discussion with the authorities concerned will also be very useful.

The main difficulty is in obtaining data for non-government institutions. If no data on teacher salaries are available for them, these may have to be estimated, as a proportion of the teacher salary of corresponding public school/college teachers.

The teachers' salaries vary not only with the level and type of education and between private and public institutions, but also with the educational and professional qualifications of teachers and the number of years of service. So the average teacher salary for a particular level and type of education has to be obtained as a weighted average of the average annual teacher salary for each category of teachers, the weights being the number in each category. In calculating the average teacher salary for each category of teachers, not only the basic pay but also the allowances paid such as house rent, cost-of-living allowance, pension and provident fund contributions, etc. have to be taken into account. It is not easy to obtain all this data from any one source but a concerted effort to collect them from various sources will generally be fruitful.

Other items of recurring costs. The individual per-pupil cost for each of the items, other than teacher cost, listed above is usually very difficult to obtain. In such cases, the per-pupil cost of those items for which data are readily available can be separately identified and the other items can be pooled together to form what can be termed as "other per-pupil cost". The sources of information are also more or less the same as listed in the case of teachers' salaries. But the main source will be the statistics on educational expenditure, and discussion with the relevant authorities who will be able to highlight the limitations of the data in expenditure statistics. Information on per-pupil cost of books supplied free, welfare cost and scholarship and stipend costs can be obtained from the relevant records of the ministries concerned. The data on the central administrative expenditure will be readily available from the budget of ministries of education.

The recurring cost components have to be calculated for each year of the simulation period, based on the data for the last year and their trends in the future. In estimating the future yearly average teacher salaries, and other costs per pupil, the likely changes in the structure of costs and also likely real increases have to be taken into account. The "other costs" in relation to teacher salary may increase as the equipment and supplies in schools are improved. The average teacher salaries may increase not only because of increases in the service of the incumbents but also because of increasing pay scales. All these factors are to be taken into account in projecting future unit costs. It is better to avoid the estimation of costs at current prices by using constant prices. It is not easy to foresee the trend of prices in the long term.

(b) <u>Capital costs</u>

As in the case of recurring costs, in determining capital costs, the basic concept is in unit terms; in this case the unit being a pupil place. The unit per-pupil-place capital cost can be divided into many components. In the model, the following components have been identified:

(i) Cost of site per unit area
(ii) Per-pupil-place area requirements for site
(iii) Cost per unit area for building teaching and common facilities
(iv) Per-pupil-place area requirements for teaching and common facilities
(v) Cost per unit area for laboratories and workshops
(vi) Cost per pupil place for furniture and equipment
(vii) Proportion of existing pupil places to be replaced every year.

As in the case of recurring costs, the above list of components of capital costs is only illustrative of the type of components which can be identified. However, the model is flexible enough, depending upon the availability of data, to have a smaller or larger number of components. To calculate capital cost, information on the number of new pupil places to be built every year is also required.

The number of new places to be built every year, classified by level and type of education, etc., will be the same as the additional number of students to be enrolled in the courses each year and can easily be calculated from the enrolment projections of the first part of the simulation. It has to be noted that the yearly new place requirements will be equal to yearly additional enrolments only on the condition that the existing system of shifts continues. If, on the other hand, a two-shift system is introduced from the existing one-shift system, then the place requirements will have to be calculated, taking this change into account. However, if there is some backlog in the construction of pupil-places in the past, then a proportion of this number has also to be added to the above to obtain the number of new places to be constructed. What proportion of the backlog is to be added depends on the period within which the backlog is to be covered and this will have to be decided in consultation with the planning authorities in the ministries of education.

The number of pupil places to be replaced depends on the "construction type" of the various school buildings and their type. To correctly calculate replacement requirements in the base year it is necessary to have the distribution of all school buildings by their life and construction type, and to have this is very rare. However, the rate of replacement can be based on the rate of replacement in the past years and its likely trend in the future. The number of new pupil places to be constructed and the rate of replacement have to be estimated for each year of the projected period.

The source of data on the components of the cost per-pupil-place are the following:

The Public Works Department and the department dealing with school buildings in the ministries of education will be the main sources of information, together with the international regional school-building institutions. From these sources it should be possible to obtain data on all components. The cost per place will vary, not only by the type and level of institution but also according to the place where the school building is constructed and also the construction type, i.e. whether the buildings to be constructed are of the permanent type or semi-permanent type, etc.

and on the materials used. The average cost per pupil-place will have to take account of these variations, by identifying the composition and weighting suitably.

The cost per place has to be projected for each year of the projection period as an input. This projected per-pupil cost has to take into account the changing norms, if any, in pupil-place requirements, including laboratories and equipment and the consequent increase in costs. It will be better to calculate the capital costs also in terms of constant prices.

By adding the total recurring cost and the total capital cost, we arrive at the total cost. Only a part of this total cost and also of total recurring and capital costs are borne by the government. The government's responsibility on these may also vary according to the level and type of education. To calculate government expenditure, the proportion of total recurring and capital costs borne by the government has to be obtained for the base year and for the past few years, to obtain the pattern of change. The likely changes in these proportions in future years are also to be ascertained. Using these proportions, the government expenditure required for each alternative educational simulation can be calculated. This, together with the available data from plans on the likely Gross National Product of the country and the likely government budget, will enable calculation of whether the simulated educational expenditure is within the possibilities of the country. This will be one way of choosing the educational alternatives, with financial restrictions.

III. Computer Application : Problems and Concepts

(a) DEFINITION OF THE DATA-PROCESSING MODEL

The mathematical model previously defined is the theory of a mechanism. A computer should be used to devise an appropriate automation for this mechanism which, in the remainder of this paper, will be called "the data-processing model".

The usefulness of the computer is enhanced if provided with specific programmes and the mechanism of carrying out a simulation is thus automatized.

The purpose of this paper is to establish the relations between mathematical and data-processing models, and to explain the problems inherent in the construction of the data-processing model, the solutions adopted during its construction, and the facilities they offer to the planner.

(b) THE DATA-PROCESSING MODEL IN RELATION TO THE MATHEMATICAL MODEL

The data-processing model must realize the purposes of the mathematical model.

At present, however, the search for a balance between the demand for teachers and the supply has not yet been incorporated. On the other hand, certain factual aspects have been introduced, e.g. changes in educational structure can be incorporated during the course of the simulation; a distinction by age between students following the same course permits the enumeration of those who have fallen behind.

The value and need for a device which permits changes in structure have already been explained but it obviously had no place in the theoretical analysis as it is wholly a matter of data-processing.

Furthermore, the data-processing model, in certain cases, reflects reality in a form much more convenient for the work of the planner, e.g. comparative tables compiled of results over ten years, the rates of growth from one year to the next, the age graphs for school enrolments and population, and the corresponding school enrolment rates. In other words, the way of representing the existing situation of the educational system and of changes in it are adapted to provide a better picture of the real situation.

Restrictions on the application of the model

As the construction of the data-processing model imposes restrictions on its absorption capacity, certain limitations were considered.

However, as far as the structure of the system is concerned, it can take up to a hundred different courses and up to ten successive different courses for the same course. In cost calculations, up to thirty aggregations of courses can be made and, in studying "cumulative school leavers" up to ten levels and twenty types for each level can be distinguished.

This sort of restriction applies to every computer use. The limits were chosen in relation to the capacity of the computer utilized (ICL 1902A) so that most of the simulation demands could be satisfied. However, should these limits become really restrictive, adjustments could be made in the data-processing model to cancel out this negative effect.

It is of course often necessary in data-processing procedures to reach a compromise between having a minimum of restrictions on programme applications and ensuring rapidity and flexibility in the computer runs.

(c) STRUCTURE OF THE DATA-PROCESSING MODEL

The data-processing model distinguishes four parts:

P1: calculation of student numbers and of teachers needed
P2: calculation of costs
P3: calculation of cumulative total of school-leavers
P4: aggregation of sub-systems.

P1: Calculation of student numbers and of teachers needed

For each simulation year, the following calculations are made: Student numbers (E_y^c) and school-leavers (0_y^c) for each course in the educational system. It should be noted that the calculation of student numbers takes account of any students who may lag behind the ideal age-group as fixed by the planner for each particular course. It is legitimate to speak of ideal age-groups in formal education but not in non-formal education, literacy, adult education or refresher courses. Here, the typical population group may be a group of a certain age or a group who, irrespective of age, share a certain quality (e.g. illiteracy). The educational system absorbs different members of the population. Each course has its typical or "ideal" population category. Hence, each year, we can define the proportion in this category entering the system at the level of its appropriate course, as well as those entering this course and belonging to the neighbouring categories (-1, +1, +2, +3, +4).

This demographic allocation allows also the calculation of the totals and of the enrolment ratios for each category of population so defined.

For each aggregation of courses (grouped on the basis of years of study, level, or types of education) the number of students (E_y^t) is calculated, the increase in relation to the previous year, and the number of teachers needed (T_y^t).

The school-leavers from each of the different courses are regrouped by type and level of education.

P2: Calculation of costs

The numbers of students and teachers needed for each aggregation of courses in P1 provide the basis for the calculation of costs.

For each simulation year, calculations are made as follows:

Current cost per student in each aggregation of courses.

For each aggregation of courses, current costs and the various costs which compose it: salaries of teachers and other staff; administrative overheads; operational and maintenance costs; books, social services (e.g. canteens); auxiliary services (e.g. transport); scholarships and grants; cost of teaching material other than books. These different calculations are optional, however, depending on whether or not the data for making them exist.

Calculation, for each aggregation of courses, of the unit cost of school places, of the number of places to be provided and the consequential capital costs.

Total cost per aggregation of courses.

Total current costs, total capital cost and total cost for the educational system.

Total cost as percentage of GNP.

Proportion of cost from public sources and relationship to total public revenues.

The relations, each year, for each of the major heads of expenditure, between expenditure for the current year and that for the first year of simulation.

P3: Calculation of cumulative total of school-leavers

The cumulative total of school-leavers shows how many have left during the years of simulation.

P1 provides the numbers of students leaving school each year, by type and level of education. These simple totals provide the basis for the cumulative totals, which give the total of all school-leavers over the years in question with due regard to certain changes that take place after schooling, and even ageing and deaths.

For the simple totals of persons of specific types and levels, the planner must find an "average age" - the presumed average age of students leaving the educational system.

The ageing factor for the simple totals is easy to calculate as their current age is defined by their average age on leaving the system and their age relative to the present school population, i.e. the number of years that have passed since they left.

The mortality factor is included by applying, each year, to each group of school-leavers the appropriate survival rate for the individuals who compose it.

Thus brought up-to-date, the simple totals are then added together to provide the cumulative totals by type and level of education, without distinction of age.

P4: Aggregation of sub-systems

Let us suppose that the planner wishes to distinguish various sub-systems within a given educational system (geographical areas, ethnic differences, sex differences, etc...). It is useful for him to be able to make studies of numbers separately for the various sub-systems and studies of costs and cumulative totals for the whole system. The results for the sub-systems found in P1 are brought together to provide the totals.

This, of course, can only be done in so far as there is compatibility between the educational structures of the different sub-systems.

The fact that this compatibility is at present defined in terms of equivalent structures does not impose any restrictions as it is always possible to define a structure (admittedly larger) which will be compatible with those of the various sub-systems.

The operation of grouping two sub-systems together can be repeated as often as may be desired to group a given number of sub-systems in one or in several combinations. This procedure takes as data the results of the P1 operations for each of the two sub-systems, these being kept on two separate tapes. P4 produces for each of the groups so formed taped results and as the structure of the information on this tape is identical to that on the other tapes the iterative aspect desired is obtained. This treatment allows any desired division into sub-systems; each sub-system may already be an assembly of still smaller sub-systems and grouping is possible at any level.

Each of the four parts whose functions have just been explained is carried out independently of the others for all of the years covered by the simulation. The only direct relations between these parts derive from the fact that the student number results (P1) serve as the basis for the "cost" calculations (P2), for the "cumulative output" (P3), and the aggregation of sub-systems (P4). Hence P1 must first be carried out before P2, P3 and P4 become possible.

To allow the various parts to be carried out independently in time, the P1 results are stored on tape.

Programmes for the data-processing model

The data-processing model consists of four programmes written in FORTRAN:

(1) a programme for P1, P2 and P3, using data on cards;
(2) an exactly similar programme, except that it takes its data from tape;
(3) a programme which, from the data on cards, makes and updates files on tape;
(4) a programme for P4.

Programmes (1) and (2) are identical except for the differences mentioned. They have a master programme and a series of sub-programmes for auxiliary functions; link-up of the parts; tape management, including labelling (name of tape); search for pseudo sub-files of data on tape for (2) above; interpretation of data; correction of errors, printing of titles.

(d) FACILITIES PROVIDED BY THE DATA-PROCESSING MODEL

The aim all through has been to make the model as practical a working tool as possible.

Form of data

The form of the data is specific to this kind of work.

The planner is a direct user. Except for the perforation of the data on cards, without any modification of form, there is no intermediary between the writing of the data and the product from the model.

To avoid submerging the user in a mass of rigid and complicated codes and formats, symbolic names and free formats are used wherever possible. With symbolic names we can identify the variable to which are allocated one or more values, represented by the number(s) which follows the symbolic name. The free formats eliminate the necessity of centring the values in the very precise columns with cards; writing is easy, the values being separated by commas, irrespective of the number of spaces which precede or follow each.

Hence, a listing of data-cards becomes a valuable working document which the user has no difficulty in understanding.

Moreover, if a group of values is identical from one year to the next, it is not necessary to repeat it the following year, this further facilitates data preparation.

Data on tape

A programme taking its data from tape represents a further step towards easier utilization.

It means less perforated cards, elimination of manual handling of the data files, totally guaranteed conservation of data - in addition to which the computer time necessary is considerably reduced.

A programme which simultaneously creates and updates data files provides a very flexible means of rectifying data. This programme allows the creation of an alternative by providing the first set of data on cards. Rectifications can, if necessary, be made in the file simply by perforating the changes. Similarly, if it is necessary to set up a second alternative patterned partially on the first, the duplication of sets of cards and delicate manual changes are avoided. The user has listings at his disposal reflecting the data and operations performed.

Detection of errors

The data-processing model must itself be able to detect any errors which may have been introduced into the data if the results are to be trustworthy.

The detection of errors is ensured in two ways. First, controls are made of the value of variables when these have boundaries (e.g. rates less than or equal to unity; a population must be a positive integer; the sum of the percentages of distribution from one course towards its successors must equal one hundred, and so on). Secondly, the error may be introduced by data which are not in their proper form: absence of expected information, presence of unwanted information. In this case as in the last, everything possible has been done to allow the model to continue while the error is being traced and notified to the user.

A "diagnostic" list, printed in clear separately from the results, makes it possible to update the data file, as explained above.

Execution of the different parts

As already indicated, the individual parts can be independently executed but they can also be linked in one simple execution procedure.

For this purpose the user has a set of parameter cards for the desired link-up. He can also automatically join up the execution of different alternatives without each of them necessarily concerning the same parts.

The possibility of running the parts through separately allows the independent preparation of the data on the different parts and so diminishes computer time, since the same P1 part has not to be re-executed for other P2 or P3 runs.

How the model is used

The preparation of an alternative starts with the perforation of data for the calculation of enrolment projections. This work is done in two parts: perforation of the first set of cards and checking by a specialized service; creation of data files - exactly reflecting the cards - on tape. The listing made in creating these files can be checked for errors made either during perforation or in transcribing data. The tape file is then corrected if necessary. The data-processing model can be executed on P1, the diagnostic, and the simulation results can be used to make a first analysis. Modifications (rectification of errors not picked up, correction of wrong values) may be made, and then one or more other executions can follow.

Once the results are considered satisfactory and the data files correct, the planner may decide - if it has not already been done meanwhile - to construct the other data files (P2, P3) and execute these parts on the model. A second set of P1 data can be made simply by modifying the previous one, so as to define a second alternative. It then becomes possible to deal simultaneously with, for example, the model for a first alternative, parts P2 and P3 (P1 already having been done), followed by a second alternative P1. It is often better to consider P1 for several alternatives before starting on P2 (costs) and P3 (cumulative output).

At this stage we can eliminate certain alternatives that give enrolment results which in themselves or in relation to others are no longer of interest. The planner can then accurately determine a set of optimal data which offer the best alternative, or retain a small number of alternatives.

Moreover, if he has decided to make a study of totals for the same country but for two or more sub-systems (by geographical areas, sex, etc.), he can group them with the aid of P4, and so calculate the costs and cumulative output for the particular groups selected.

It should be noted that a very accurate set of parameter cards must be provided for the model so as to indicate which data files are to be used and which parts the model is to execute.

These parameters are: the name of the country (it is possible to consider several countries at the same time), the number of the alternative, the sub-system indicator (for the data), and the number(s) of the parts to be executed.

Once these parameters are fed in, the model establishes a dialogue with the person in charge in the computer room, and requests whatever data tapes are needed; the special tape containing the P1 results for subsequent runs with other parts; and another tape for storing results reflected in the listing supplied to the planner.

Form of the results

In view of their numbers, the results must be easy to handle and be rationally displayed so as to simplify analysis by the planner.

The "diagnostic" list is in itself a result in the sense of providing a check on proper execution by the model for the alternative selected. For easier use, it is listed separately from the main results.

The main results are recorded on tape (off-lining); this saves time and allows the preservation and subsequent printing of any number of copies of the results.

The listings so obtained are very clearly presented. The heading gives the date, the country, the number of the alternative and the sub-system simulated. The results for the different parts are listed separately, each under its appropriate title.

For each part the results are displayed year by year. Some results are optional, depending on the parameters the user has chosen.

Study of the alternative is simplified by the presence on the same listing of the data which have defined the system and its evolution, facing the results they have produced. Depending on the case, data and results may be shown in the same table, or on the same page so as to bring out the relations between cause and effect.

Certain aspects of the state of the educational system are illustrated by graphs (enrolments, population by age) as well as being expressed in figures.

To give a clearer idea of how the system changes over a period of years, recapitulatory tables for the selected years are automatically printed after the execution of P1; they give values for key variables, e.g. number of pupils per course; increase in enrolment per course; number of pupils, enrolment ratios and increase in numbers by age; numbers and increases for various aggregations of courses, and the teachers necessary for each such aggregation.

The planner can obtain similar tables for other years without having to execute P1 again.

The synthesis can also be made after the execution of P4 in order to obtain the corresponding aggregation of sub-systems.

(e) FUTURE DEVELOPMENTS OF THE MODEL

Two possible types of development concern (1) the way in which a country simulation is carried out, and (2) extensions of the use of the model in education.

(1) Improvement of the simulation

It would be an improvement if the model were fed statistical data in the form in which they are communicated to the planner.

All statistics offices provide demographic forecasts for years ending in 0 and 5, whereas simulation requires figures for each year. Interpolations are at present calculated on office machines; they could be introduced into the model itself, thus reducing the work to be done before the simulation.

It would also be interesting to generalize the practice of furnishing the data via a minimum of information by communicating one or more values and a variation law.

Once a simulation has been made for a country, it could be repeated one or more years later, to check on the practical implementation of the plan of education and introduce whatever adjustments seem necessary in the plan.

Special arrangements would be necessary to permit this. It would operate with the old data of the model and the data on the new state of the educational system. Statistical data should therefore be assembled and conserved on permanent files.

To facilitate the comparative analysis of two sub-systems, separately and together, P4 should simultaneously print the appropriate results in parallel on the same listing.

At present the publication of the results at the end of a simulation demands a great deal of work on their presentation and it would be useful to get nearer to the final form of presentation.

Standardized formats usable for all countries are unfortunately impossible because of the great variations of the educational systems.

To obtain the printing directly in the desired form in the absence of standardization, a special programme could be devised to which all the results of the alternatives would be fed - but it would be very complicated.

To allow more rapid decision-making by the planner, it would be interesting to define and print the minimum of general results necessary to represent schematically the state and evolution of the educational system and of its environment. This would in no way prevent the planner, if he so desired from subsequently studying the more detailed results provided by the listing.

The planner could similarly be helped to obtain a rapid, comprehensive view of possible changes in the educational system. A set of most important data could be provided by amalgamation from the present model, e.g. all the data regrouped by level and type of education.

This "mini model" should be formally worked out and should permit dialogue with the user, allowing him, at will, to define the data, start the simulation, control it and obtain the results he requires.

(2) Extensions of the model's use in education

The notion of strategic courses can be introduced into the model to provide a check on distribution of the student flow, through limits (lower or upper), imposed on the enrolment in the "strategic" courses.

This can be done by readjustment of the flow rates from certain courses towards the strategic courses. A first, non-adjusted simulation will allow an evaluation of the "strategic" enrolments possible.

To the extent to which the theoretical basis for calculating the number of teachers available has been generalized, it will be possible to consider adjustments with a view to achieving a balance between the demand for teachers and the supply.

Some of these adjustments affect the P1 calculations, e.g. the numbers of future teachers.

In general, the adjustments are made by first doing the preliminary calculations and then analysing the results, mainly in relation to key conditions, so as to define the modifications which will then be made.

So if "teacher equilibrium" is integrated into the present model, it will be necessary to calculate the number of teachers available, see what constitutes equilibrium, and what adjustments[1] are needed each year.

Certain results obtained on manpower, costs or population by level of education may require readjustment of the enrolments. This would demand a different structure for the model, since it must be possible to link up each of the different parts year by year.

Similarly, conditions and associated adjustments should preferably be separable for periods greater than one year of simulation, so that account can be taken of the natural inertia of certain aspects of the educational system in making the readjustments. In short, these adjustments allow the user to trace and follow changes in the educational system which derive not only from the model's own parameters but also from conditions that affect the desired results. They must be made in relation to the parameters which define the variables they affect, their use must be optional.

Data-processing aspects of these developments

All improvements that concern data, results, readjustments even within P1, and the calculations of population by level of education, may lead to modifications in the present model.

---

[1] i.e. Modification of the ratios and consequential changes in calculations to which they relate. In this particular case, they may influence the calculations of the enrolment for the teacher-training courses and of the numbers of teachers required.

However, some of the proposed developments would demand structural innovations: adjustments as between the parts and in the global model as a whole.

There is no problem in writing a model which allows adjustments between the parts. The links between the parts are simply managed differently but this does affect the structure of the data, i.e. the way in which they are arranged in the memory and subsequent access when they are being treated.

The problem is different when the adjustments relate to years already simulated. There are great difficulties in making re-runs from the model while it is being executed; and a trace of the complete state of the system must be stored for each year. However, the writing of recursive procedures could help to solve this double problem of re-start and memorizing.[1]

Reference has already been made to the advantages of a global study model of an alternative and of a model with which the planner can have a dialogue. For such a dialogue, appropriate computer equipment must be available - such accessories as a tele-printer or screen.

The writing of programmes for this new model must thus be such as to allow the possibility of dialogue and the execution of the programme should be under the direct control of the user. The model will behave as a robot to which various types of questions can be put and will involve: (i) input of data with visualization; (ii) start of the simulation for a specific number of years and request for particular outputs.

(i) <u>Input of data: constitution of data files</u>. Regardless of the type of data, the planner can constitute the files required for the model simply by typing the values on the keyboard after first selecting a function (e.g. typing of a code) which allows the model to recognize all the information relevant to the proper interpretation of these values. What he types appears on the screen and he can make any corrections necessary before typing a last code which leads to the execution of the function specified on the values expressed.

It is also possible to modify existing files. To do so, the user gives a function which defines the set of data on which he wishes to operate, asks for visualization, specifies the value(s) to be modified, types the modifications and follows with the "execution" code. A print-out of the files which the planner has just constituted can be conserved: a print function can be requested and a listing printed of the values of the data relating to the file printed.

(ii) <u>Start of the simulation and visualization of the results</u>. Execution proceeds step by step, i.e. year by year. At the outset, the user specifies the number of years of simulation he desires but maintains control of the simulation and can suspend execution if the results at the end of the simulation for a year are not correct. He can then visualize the files which might have caused these anomalies, or ask for the screening of all the comparative tables for the various years since the first year of simulation.

Following the procedures indicated in the preceding paragraph, the user can make corrections and start executing the model again as from the year he specifies to it.

All the results for the previous years are kept including those for the year immediately preceding which constitute the data for the initial year in this new execution.

The model also deals with the presence or absence of the data required for its execution. Once the planner has started the simulation, the model stops if the data for a particular year are missing, and a message appears on the screen. The files needed for the simulation can be constituted and the model starts again from where it stopped.

The visualization of the results must be clear and the associated instructions varied. It should then be possible to obtain graphs of the enrolments for one simulation year and, from a single instruction, to obtain those for the following year. This possibility of obtaining comparisons for the different years of simulation should be extended to all the tables of simulation results. In addition, when he has viewed the results, the user can conserve a listing print-out - this, of course, being optional.

After his general study, the planner should be allowed to make more refined simulations, and so establish the refined data equivalent of the general data.

In doing so, he should be aided by conversational (interactive) programmes. This group of programmes would effectively extend the mini-model described earlier.

Used conversationally, the global model could thus be a practical instrument for the direct and rapid preparation of an alternative for the purposes of making a more objective simulation that would give more refined results.

(1 Recursive procedures can be employed in advanced algorithmic language (ALGOL) for solving such problems.

UNESCO PUBLICATIONS: NATIONAL DISTRIBUTORS

Argentina	Editorial Losada, S.A., Alsina 1131, BUENOS AIRES.
Australia	*Publications:* Educational Supplies Pty. Ltd., Box 33, Post Office BROOKVALE 2100, N.S.W. *Periodicals:* Dominie Pty. Ltd., Box 33, Post Office, BROOKVALE 2100, N.S.W. *Sub-agent:* United Nations Association of Australia (Victorian Division), 5th Floor, 134-136 Flinders St., MELBOURNE 3000.
Austria	Verlag Georg Fromme & Co., Arbeitergasse 1-7, 1051 WIEN.
Belgium	Jean De Lannoy, 112, rue du Trône, BRUXELLES 5.
Bolivia	Librería Universitaria, Universidad San Francisco Xavier, apartado 212, SUCRE.
Brazil	Fundação Getúlio Vargas, Serviço de Publicações, caixa postal 21120 Praia de Botafogo 183, RIO DE JANEIRO, G.B.
Bulgaria	Hemus, Kantora Literatura, bd. Rousky 6, SOFIJA.
Burma	Trade Corporation n.° (9), 550-552 Merchant Street, RANGOON.
Cameroon	Le Secrétaire général de la Commission nationale de la République fédérale du Cameroun pour l'Unesco, B.P. 1061, YAOUNDÉ.
Canada	Information Canada, OTTAWA (Ont.).
Chile	Editorial Universitaria, S.A., casilla 10220, SANTIAGO.
Colombia	Librería Buccholz Galeria, avenida Jiménez de Quesada 8-40, apartado aéreo 49-56, BOGOTÁ; Distrilibros Ltda., Pío Alfonso García, carrera 4ª, nº 36-119 y 36-125, CARTAGENA; J. Germán Rodríguez N., Calle 17, 6-59, apartado nacional 83, GIRARDOT (Cundinamarca). Editorial Losada Ltda. Calle 18A n.° 7-37, apartado aéreo 5829, apartado nacional 931, BOGOTÁ. *Sub-depots:* Edificio La Ceiba, Oficina 804, MEDELLÍN; Calle 37, n.° 14-73 Oficina, 305, BUCARAMANGA; Edificio Zaccour, Oficina 736, CALI.
Congo	Librairie populaire, B.P. 577, BRAZZAVILLE.
Costa Rica	Librería Trejos S.A., apartado 1313, SAN JOSÉ. Teléfonos: 2285 y 3200.
Cuba	Distribuidora Nacional de Publicaciones, Neptuno 674, LA HABANA.
Cyprus	'MAM', Archbishop Makarios 3rd Avenue, P.O. Box 1722, NICOSIA.
Czechoslovakia	SNTL, Spalena 51, PRAHA 1 *(Permanent display)*; Zahranicni literatura, 11 Soukenicka, PRAHA 1. *For Slovakia only:* Alfa Verlag Publishers Hurbanovo nam. 6, 893 31 BRATISLAVA.
Dahomey	Librairie nationale, B.P. 294, PORTO NOVO.
Denmark	Ejnar Munksgaard Ltd., 6 Nørregade, 1165 KØBENHAVN K.
Egypt	Librairie Kasr El Nil, 38, rue Kasr El Nil, LE CAIRE. National Centre for Unesco Publications 1 Tlaat Harb Street, Tahrir Square, CAIRO.
Ethiopia	National Commission for Unesco, P.O. Box 2996, ADDIS ABABA.
Finland	Akateeminen Kirjakauppa 2 Keskuskatu, HELSINKI.
France	Librairie de l'Unesco, 7 place de Fontenoy, 75700 PARIS. CCP 12598-48.
French West Indies	Librairie 'Au Boul' Mich', 1 Rue Perrinon and 66 Avenue du Parquet, 972 FORT-DE-FRANCE (Martinique).
German Dem. Rep.	Deutscher Buch-Export und -Import GmbH Leninstrasse 16, 701 LEIPZIG.
Fed. Rep. of Germany	Verlag Dokumentation, Postfach 148, Jaiserstrasse 13, 8023, MÜNCHEN-PULLACH. 'The Courier' *(German edition only)*: Bahrenfelder Chaussee 160, HAMBURG-BAHRENFELD. CCP 27 66 50.
Ghana	Presbyterian Bookshop Depot Ltd., P.O. Box 195, ACCRA; Ghana Book Suppliers Ltd., P.O. Box 7869, ACCRA; The University Bookshop of Ghana, ACCRA; The University Bookshop of Cape Coast; The University Bookshop of Legon, P.O. Box 1, LEGON.
Greece	Anglo-Hellenic Agency, 5 Koumpari Street, ATHINAI 138.
Hong Kong	Swindon Book Co., 13-15 Lock Road, KOWLOON.
Hungary	Akadémiai Könyvesbolt Váci u 22, BUDAPEST V. A.K.V. Könyvtárosok Boltja, Népköztársaság utja 16, BUDAPEST VI.
Iceland	Snaebjörn Jonsson & Co. H. F., Hafnarstracti 9, REYKJAVIK.
India	Orient Longman Ltd.; Nicol Road, Ballard Estate, BOMBAY 1; 17 Chittaranjan Avenue, CALCUTTA 13; 36A Anna Salai, Mount Road, MADRAS 2; B-3/7 Asaf Ali Road, NEW DELHI 1. *Sub-depots:* Oxford Book & Stationery Co., 17 Park Street, CALCUTTA 16; *and* Scindia House, NEW DELHI; Publications Section, Ministry of Education and Youth Services, 72 Theatre Communication Building, Connaught Place, NEW DELHI 1.
Indonesia	Indira P.T., Jl. Dr. Sam Ratulangie 37, JAKARTA.
Iran	Commission nationale iranienne pour l'Unesco, avenue Iranchahr Chomali nº 300, B.P. 1533, TÉHÉRAN. Kharazmie Publishing and Distribution Co., 229 Daneshgahe Street, Shah Avenue, P.O. Box 14/1486, TÉHÉRAN.
Iraq	McKenzie's Bookshop, Al-Rashid Street, BAGHDAD; University Bookstore, University of Baghdad, P.O. Box 75, BAGHDAD.
Ireland	The National Press, 2 Wellington Road, Ballsbridge, DUBLIN 4.
Israel	Emanuel Brown, formerly Blumstein's Bookstores: 35 Allenby Road *and* 48 Nachlat Benjamin Street, TEL AVIV; 9 Shlomzion Hamalka Street, JERUSALEM.
Italy	LICOSA (Libreria Commissionaria Sansoni S.p.A.), via Lamarmora 45, casella postale 552, 50121 FIRENZE.
Jamaica	Sangster's Book Stores Ltd., P.O. Box 366, 101 Water Lane, KINGSTON.
Japan	Maruzen Co. Ltd., P.O. Box 5050, Tokyo International, TOKYO.
Kenya	The ESA Ltd., P.O. Box 30167, NAIROBI.
Khmer Republic	Librarie Albert Portail, 14, avenue Boulloche, PHNOM-PENH.
Republic of Korea	Korean National Commission for Unesco, P.O. Box Central 64, SEOUL.
Kuwait	The Kuwait Bookshop Co. Ltd., P.O. Box 2942, KUWAIT.
Liberia	Cole & Yancy Bookshops Ltd., P.O. Box 286, MONROVIA.
Libya	Agency for Development of Publication and Distribution, P.O. Box 34-35, TRIPOLI.
Luxembourg	Librairie Paul Bruck, 22 Grande-Rue, LUXEMBOURG.
Malaysia	Federal Publications Sdn. Bhd., Balai Berita, 31 Jalan Riong, KUALA LUMPUR.
Malta	Sapienza's Library, 26 Kingsway, VALLETTA.
Mauritius	Nalanda Co. Ltd, 30 Bourbon Street, PORT-LOUIS.
Mexico	CILA (Centra Interamericano de Libros Académicos), Sullivan 31 *bis*, MÉXICO 4, D.F.
Monaco	British Library, 30, boulevard des Moulins, MONTE-CARLO.
Netherlands	N.V. Martinus Nijhoff, Lange Voorhout 9, 's-GRAVENHAGE; Systemen Keesing, Ruysdaelstraat 71-75, AMSTERDAM.
Netherlands Antilles	G. C. T. Van Dorp & Co. (Ned. Ant.) N.V., WILLEMSTAD (Curaçao, N.A.).
New Caledonia	Reprex S.A.R.L., B.P. 1572, NOUMÉA.
New Zealand	Government Printing Office, Government Bookshops: Rutland Street, P.O. Box 5344, AUCKLAND; 130 Oxford Terrace, P.O. Box 1721, CHRISTCHURCH; Alma Street, P.O. Box 857, HAMILTON; Princes Street, P.O. Box 1104, DUNEDIN; Mulgrave Street, Private Bag, WELLINGTON.
Niger	Librairie Manclert, B.P. 868, NIAMEY.
Nigeria	The University Bookshop of Ife; The University Bookshop of Ibadan, P.O. Box 286, IBADAN; The University of Nsukka; The University Bookshop of Lagos; The Ahmadu Bello University Bookshop of Zaria.
Norway	*All publications:* Johan Grundt Tanum, Karl Johans gate 41/43, OSLO 1. 'The Courier' *only:* A/S Narvesens Litteraturtjeneste, Box 6125, OSLO 6.
Pakistan	The West-Pak Publishing Co. Ltd., Unesco Publications House, P.O. Box 374, G.P.O., LAHORE. *Showrooms:* Urdu Bazaar, LAHORE and 57-58 Murree Highway, G/6-1, ISLAMABAD. Pakistan Publications Bookshop: Sarwar Road, RAWALPINDI; Mirza Book Agency, 65 Shahrah Quaid-e-azam P.O. Box 729 LAHORE 3.
Peru	*'The Courier' only:* Editorial Losada Peruana, apartado 472, LIMA. *Other publications:* Distribuidora Inca S.A., Emilio Althaus 470, Lince, casilla 3115, LIMA.
Philippines	The Modern Book Co., 926 Rizal Avenue, P.O. Box 632, MANILA.
Poland	Osrodek Rozpowzechniania Wydawnictw Naukowych PAN, Palac Kultury i Nauki, WARSZAWA.
Portugal	Dias & Andrade Ltda., Libraria Portugal, rua o Carmo 70, LISBOA.
Southern Rhodesia	Textbook Sales (PVT) Ltd., 67 Union Avenue, SALISBURY.
Romania	I.C.E. LIBRI, Calea Victoriei, nr. 126, P.O. Box 134-135 BUCUREŞTI. *Subscriptions to periodicals:* Rompresfilatelia, Calea Victoriei nr. 29, BUCUREŞTI.
Senegal	La Maison du Livre, 13, avenue Roume, B.P. 20-60, DAKAR; Librairie Clairafrique, B.P. 2005, DAKAR; Librairie 'Le Sénégal', B.P. 1594, DAKAR.

Singapore	Federal Publications Sdn Bhd., Times House, River Valley Road, SINGAPORE 9
South Africa	Van Schaik's Bookstore (Pty.) Ltd., Libri Building, Church Street, P.O. Box 7.24, PRETORIA.
Spain	*All publications*: Editiones Iberoamericanas, S.A., calle de Oñate 15, MADRID 20; Distribución de Publicaciones del Consejo Superior de Investigaciones Científicas, Vitrubio 16, MADRID 6; Librería del Consejo Superior de Investigaciones Científicas, Egigcíacas 15, BARCELONA. *For 'The Courier' only*: Ediciones Liber, apartado 17, ONDÁRROA (Viscaya).
Sri Lanka	Lake House Bookshop, Sir Chittampalam Gardiner Mawata, P.O. Box 244, COLOMBO 2.
Sudan	Al Bashir Bookshop, P.O. Box 1118, KHARTOUM.
Sweden	*All publications*: A/BC.E. Fritzes Kungl. Hovbokhandel, Fredsgatan 2, Box 16356, 103 27 STOCKHOLM 16. *For 'The Courier'*: Svenska FN-Förbundet, Skolgränd 2, Box 150 50, S-104 65 STOCKHOLM.
Switzerland	Europa Verlag, Rämistrasse 5, ZÜRICH; Librairie Payot, 6, rue Grenus, 1211 GENÈVE 11.
Tanzania	Dar es Salaam Bookshop, P.O. Box 9030, DAR ES SALAAM.
Thailand	Suksapan Panit, Mansion 9, Rajdamnern Avenue, BANGKOK.
Togo	Librairie évangélique, B.P. 378; LOMÉ; Librairie du Bon Pasteur, B.P. 1164, LOMÉ; Librairie moderne B.P.777, LOMÉ.
Turkey	Librairie Hachette, 469 Istiklal Caddesi, Beyoglu, ISTANBUL.
Uganda	Uganda Bookshop, P.O. Box 145, KAMPALA.
U.S.S.R.	Mezhdunarodnaja Kniga, MOSKVA, G-200.
United Kingdom	H.M. Stationery Office, P.O. Box 569, LONDON SE1 9NH; Government bookshops: London, Belfast, Birmingham, Bristol, Cardiff, Edinburgh, Manchester.
United States	Unesco Publications Center, P.O. Box 433, New York, N.Y. 10016.
Upper Volta	Librairie Attie. B.P. 64, Ouagadougou, Librairie catholique 'Jeunesse d'Afrique', OUAGADOUGOU.
Venezuela	Librería Historia, Monjas a Padre Sierra, Edificio Oeste 2, n.º 6 (frente al Capitolio), apartadode correos 7320-101, CARACAS.
Yugoslavia	Jugoslovenska Knjiga, Terazije 27, BEOGRAD. Drzavna Zalozba Slovenije Mestni Trg. 26, LJUBLJANA.
Zaire	La Librairie, Institut national d'études politiques, B.P. 2307, KINSHASA; Commission nationale de la République du Zaïre pour l'Unesco, Ministère de l'éducation nationale, KINSHASA.